THE DROPOUT PREVENTION HANDBOOK

A Guide for Administrators, Counselors, and Teachers

Nancy Conover Myll

PARKER PUBLISHING COMPANY
West Nyack, New York 10995

10 9 8 7 6 5 4 3 2 1

> *For dad, whose faith and support*
> *inspired me to write this book.*

Library of Congress Cataloging-in-Publication Data

Myll, Nancy Conover.
  The dropout prevention handbook : a guide for administrators,
counselors, and teachers / Nancy Conover Myll.
     p. cm.
  Includes index.
  ISBN 0-13-220799-0
  1. High school dropouts—Services for—United States—Handbooks,
manuals, etc. I. Title.
LC146.5.M95 1988
373.12'913—dc19   88-22832
                                                                CIP

ISBN 0-13-220799-0

PARKER PUBLISHING COMPANY
BUSINESS & PROFESSIONAL DIVISION
A division of Simon & Schuster
West Nyack, New York 10995

Printed in the United States of America

About the Author

Nancy C. Myll is a teacher at the Center for Independent Study, an individualized alternative high school with a diversified student body that includes special need students such as students in need of remedial help, gifted students, teenage parents, pregnant minors, drug rehabilitation patients, students discharged from mental health units, public assistance recipients, foster youths, reluctant learners, continuation students, dropouts, General Educational Development candidates, and adults. She also serves on the Dropout/At Risk Student Task committee of the San Juan (California) Unified School District.

She holds a Life Standard Teaching Credential from the state of California and a Masters of Science in Education Administration with a preliminary Administrative Service Credential. She has completed various classes in counseling techniques, Carkhuff training, and peer group pressures. She worked as a counselor in an adolescent health clinic that was funded through a federal grant.

Myll is a member of the California Learning Alternatives Resource Network and the California Consortium of Independent Study (CCIS) and served two years as a region representative for CCIS, chairing two innovative and effective region conferences. She has received service awards for conference and workshop presentations and acknowledgment for her volunteer services on the committee to update and revise the California State Independent Study Manual.

She has participated in the development of dropout prevention programs and spent several years attending weekly administrative meetings to review student cases for referral to alternative programs. She has taught for four years in traditional classrooms and for ten years in various alternative programs.

Acknowledgments

I owe special thanks to those who have contributed to the development of this book. I appreciate the discussions, interviews, and extra materials provided to me by specialists who work in dropout prevention programs. The individuals acknowledged were helpful, but are in no way responsible for any faults or limitations in this book. The final product is a result of my interpretation of the facts about programs. The case histories are my own.

Sincere thanks to Ann Stewart, counselor, Sacramento County Community Schools; Bob Mikesell, ROP-OWE coordinator, San Juan Unified School District Sacramento; and Marta Reyes, Director of Community Home Schooling, El Dorado County, for donating their time to provide me with an interview and a tour of the facilities.

I am grateful to Dr. Lynn Hartzler, High Risk Youth Liaison, California Department of Education, who patiently answered my questions and provided me with an abundance of referrals, and to Ray Eberhard, program manager for high risk youth, California Department of Education, who reviewed my outline and offered suggestions to enhance the manuscript.

I am indebted to Newell Herum of the Visalia Unified School District, who had faith in my ability to help start a new program. My sincere appreciation to Dr. Harry Rosenburg of the Visalia Unified School District and to Ken Sherer, Director of Continuing Education of the San Juan Unified School District, Sacramento, who provided me with materials and information that were extremely useful.

I am also indebted to Carole Parkins, program director, Center for Independent Study, San Juan Unified School District, who offered her support and continual understanding during the three years I worked under her supervision and wrote this book.

A special thank-you to the following for permission to use or adapt their forms:

- Butte County Home Study Program, Oroville, California, for Forms 12-3, 12-4, and 12-5
- California Department of Education, Independent Study State Manual, Sacramento, California, for Forms 4-1 and 4-7
- El Dorado County Office of Education, Prescription Educational Programs, Placerville, California, for Forms 12-1 and 12-2
- El Monte (California) Union High School District for Forms 5-2 and 5-3

- Sacramento (California) County Community Schools for the forms in Chapter 7

- Sacramento (California) County Office of Education, Regional Occupational Program, for the forms in Chapter 6

- San Juan Unified School District, Sacramento, California, for the forms in Chapters 1 and 6 and for Forms 3-1, 3-2, 3-3, and 4-2 through 4-5

- Visalia (California) Unified School District for the forms in Chapter 2 and Form 13-2

My thanks to the staff at Prentice-Hall, Inc., and editor Evelyn Fazio, who took a chance on my first book and offered her continued support.

And, finally, I wish to acknowledge my husband, Peter, and my children, Nicki and Guy, who endured with patience my hours away from them . . . and my father Joseph A. Conover, for his suggestions and perceptions that greatly enhanced the manuscript. And Mom . . . for understanding.

About This Handbook

The Dropout Prevention Handbook will help counselors, administrators, and teachers guide teenage students who are having trouble adjusting to the pressures of attending classes. It describes fourteen public school programs that can be used, in part or as a whole, for dropout prevention. Available at little additional cost to the school district, these programs can be established by using the guidelines suggested in this book. They can be varied as needed, depending on local conditions and environment.

The last few years have seen a proliferation of these prevention and recovery programs in the United States, principally because of the attention that has been focused on truancy, the need to get young people back in school, and the desire of school districts everywhere to reclaim lost funding from state budgets. These programs reach out to young people who are not in school and try to bring them back into the fold.

Dropout prevention programs are designed to help those unfortunate students who are affected by drug abuse, premature pregnancy, child molestation, and parental abuses of all kinds, as well as victims of accidents and other traumas who can no longer attend regular or traditional high school. These programs help stop at-risk youth from dropping out of school by providing an avenue of alternative education that meets their special needs.

Dropout retrieval programs are targeted at youth and adults who left the school system without graduating. These programs are designed to draw dropouts back into the educational folds by offering an alternative method of instruction that leads to a diploma.

This guide provides solutions to common dropout-related problems and demonstrates how various kinds of help can be made available through the public school system. It sets out formulas for implementing the programs including:

- how to identify a target population
- which contact people can help provide funding, write guidelines, and develop procedures
- what kind of reception or reaction can be expected from the community
- an outline of responsibilities for the administrators, the educators, and the youngsters who are served

More than forty-five ready-to-use forms are included that can be easily adapted to your particular needs. There is also a survey chart showing which programs are functioning in sample districts of each state of the continental United States (see Chapter 13). It demonstrates that many districts have implemented alternative forms of education to help reduce their dropout rate.

Many school districts have a surplus of "helping programs." These programs are designed merely to bring youths back to school with nothing more than a hope for the best. However, by making a few small changes, existing programs can be tailored for dropout prevention. This handbook will show you how.

Officials of dropout prevention programs usually make an evaluation of the student to determine why he or she is not attending school and then attempt to offer an arrangement that will match the student's needs. Many dropouts need a curriculum that fits their situations. A change of environment is often necessary to help prevent the original situation from recurring.

If we are to reclaim young people who are at risk of dropping out or who have already dropped out, we must seek new avenues to satisfy their needs and try whatever new techniques are available to keep them in school.

Nancy Conover Myll

SUMMARY CHART

An overview of programs discussed in the book.

Program Name	Funding Source	Age Served	Target Population	Suggested Housing	Suggested Staffing
Community School	A.D.A. state funds, county funds, sch. dist. funds	five to adult	wards of the court, abuse victims, runaways	county juvenile hall, storefront, county office	practiced teachers who have counseling background, ratio 1–20
Continuation School	A.D.A. state allocated, sch. dist. funds	fourteen to eighteen	youth at-risk for dropping out, truants	school site	practiced teachers, ratio 1–25
contract independent study	A.D.A. state allocated, sch. dist. funds	five to adult	students needing an alternate to the traditional school	school site	regular staff, ratio 1–30, one-on-one lessons
external diploma	A.D.A. state allocated, sch. dist. funds	adults	adult dropouts	school site, storefront	regular staff, ratio 1–30
General Education Development Test	sch. dist. funds	adults	adult dropouts	school site	regular staff, ratio/use district guidelines
home study	A.D.A. state allocated, sch. dist. funds	five to fourteen	home-schooled youth	school site, county offices	regular staff, ratio 1–30
Learning Opportunity	A.D.A. state allocated, sch. dist. funds	eleven to fourteen	youth at-risk for dropping out	school site	practiced teachers, ratio 1–15
parenting	A.D.A. state funds, sch. dist. funds	thirteen to eighteen	school-age parents	school site, storefront, county offices	teachers with child development background, ratio 1–25
pregnant minors	A.D.A. state funds, sch. dist. funds	thirteen to eighteen	pregnant school-age youth	school site, storefront	teachers with child development background, ratio 1–25
Regional Occupational	county	fourteen to eighteen	youth at-risk for dropping out	job sites, county offices	teacher-qualified work experience coordinator
Restart	sch. dist. funds, grants	adults	adult dropouts	school site, storefront	regular staff, ratio 1–30
School Attendance Review Board	sch. dist. funds	five to adult	truants	school board room, media center, school library	1 educator 1 parent 1 principal 1 counselor 1 board member
special education	A.D.A. state funds, grants	five to eighteen	mentally handicapped	school site	teachers trained to work with mentally handicapped
vocational education	grants, A.D.A. state funds, sch. dist. funds	fourteen to eighteen	youth at-risk for dropping out	school site	regular staff, volunteers, community entrepreneurs

Contents

Chapter Seven: MAKING USE OF COMMUNITY SCHOOLS TO HELP AT-RISK YOUNGSTERS CONTINUE THEIR EDUCATION..111

Forms

Chapter Eight: HOW OPPORTUNITY PROGRAMS MOTIVATE FAILING STUDENTS TO ACHIEVE....................................... 129

The Purpose of a School Attendance Review Board in Dropout Prevention

In spite of the notoriety given to the proliferation of drugs, alcohol, and vandalism in the public schools, student truancy is the biggest problem and by far the most costly in time consumption and expense.

Some measure of control of young students can be maintained if they can be kept in the classroom and interested in other supervised campus activities. However, truant students are more or less "free agents," going where they want, doing what they please, and spreading corruption and dissatisfaction among the more conscientious students who are attending school regularly.

In many cases, the fault arises through lack of parental supervision. Some parents simply do not take enough interest in their children's activities to be able to recognize a change in normal behavioral patterns that could be the first warning sign that their son or daughter may be playing hooky from school.

Although truancy is more prevalent after the age of twelve, the truant person may be any age.

States that require students to remain in school until the age of eighteen usually have greater problems with truancy. There are a number of reasons for this, chief among them the fact that as adolescents approach maturity they begin to want to think and act for themselves.

Strangely, many parents feel that the responsibility for keeping children in attendance belongs solely to the school system. It often comes as a complete surprise to the parent when the first phone call or letter arrives from the administrator outlining the student's absentee record and requesting that the parent, together with the student, appear at an attendance review meeting.

ADMINISTRATIVE STEPS TO TRUANCY CONTROL

It is a good idea for the school administration to establish a set policy or procedure that will encourage the parent to become involved when a student is habitually or repeatedly absent. This procedure should include, along with any other local requirements, these steps:

1. Notifying the parent by phone
2. Sending a letter that apprises the parent of the status of the problem and outlines what further action will be taken if the situation does not improve (see Form 1–1 at the end of this chapter for further guidelines)
3. Attempting, by phone or letter, to arrange a conference to help resolve the causes of the truancy (see Form 1–2 at the end of this chapter for further guidelines)
4. Sending a follow-up letter that explains the compulsory school attendance law in the state in which the school functions

When none of the above procedures alleviate the truancy problem, another alternative is needed. Some states have provided for a school attendance review board, which helps the local administration investigate possible ways of improving the attendance and behavior of the truant student. Meeting with the board is mandatory for both parent and student. Failure to attend the meeting results in referral to local law authorities.

THE SCHOOL ATTENDANCE REVIEW BOARD

A School Attendance Review Board (SARB) is a group of educators, parents, and representatives of the school district who help students and parents explore ways to resolve school attendance and behavior problems. This committee gets involved after the school personnel have made a maximum effort to do the job themselves. The SARB decides on a course of action that will assist the family with its problem. The committee functions as a consultant service and explains options that may help, such as:

1. Community resources, including abuse centers, counseling services, drug rehabilitation centers, and social security and welfare offices
2. Alternative education programs within the school system, including independent study, pregnant minors, and any others that are available.

3. A reduction in school program load, such as taking only afternoon classes, or changing from six classes a day to four

4. An intradistrict transfer to another nearby school

STAFFING THE SCHOOL ATTENDANCE REVIEW BOARD

The board should be composed of teachers, educators, counselors, parents, and administrators of the school district or community, or, more precisely, of the school the student attends. Though the board's composition may vary, it should be designed to perform essentially the same function described above. Members of this committee are recruited through a variety of means.

1. Teachers and counselors are generally selected by principals on the basis of performance, stability, educational background, and job flexibility.

2. County probation departments and welfare departments may volunteer a representative.

3. The Parent-Teacher Association at each school in the district can recommend parents who are knowledgeable about school rules and willing to donate their time.

4. The county superintendent of schools may volunteer a representative.

GUIDELINES ARE SET BY STATE LAW

State education codes that provide for attendance review boards usually determine the departments or agencies that are required to participate. Each of these agencies or departments is required to assign personnel to represent it on a continuing basis. It is a wise move to check your state education codes relating to truancy to determine which agencies and departments are involved. Should there be no relevant education code in your state, you may want to follow the guidelines in Chapter 13 to initiate legislation.

OPTIONS FOR MEETING SITES

It is not necessary to find new quarters to house a school attendance review meeting. The most common locations for a meeting are:

1. The school board room at the district office

2. The school library

3. A public library or media center

4. A classroom

5. Other meeting facilities at the school

Since only one family is seen at a time, it is advisable to provide a waiting area for families waiting their turn.

HOW LONG ARE ATTENDANCE MEETINGS?

It is impossible to predict how long a meeting will last because each case is handled individually. Depending on the number of cases on the agenda, a meeting may last from one to five hours. Meetings usually take place in the evening, but are occasionally scheduled during a school day, especially if the agenda includes suspension cases.

Parents who work outside the home often object to a lengthy daytime meeting.

THE ORDER OF BUSINESS AT A SARB MEETING

At the meeting, the participants review the student's record and discuss possible reasons for the student's behavior. Finding the underlying causes often results in a resolution. (Later on in this chapter, we will consider a case history that emphasizes some of these reasons.) Corrections or adjustments that may reestablish the student's regular school attendance are recommended. Parents and guardians are asked to help find solutions to the truancy problem. Before a student leaves the meeting, the possible solution to the problem is written in a contract that is signed by both parent and student.

FOLLOW-UP DOCUMENTATION

Following the meeting, it is wise to send a formal letter to the parents. This letter should contain a statement of the probable cause of the truancy and a report on the outcome of the meeting, plus any other information pertinent to the requirements of the state statutes that govern the school attendance of minors. It is a good idea to explain that if the student continues to be absent from school, the school officials will have to notify the juvenile authorities. This serves as a warning to the parents that any reluctance to discipline or regain control of their offspring will bring outside law enforcement authorities into the picture. An excerpt from your state's code relating to public school truancy should be included (see Form 1–1). All states have similar laws.

WHO SHOULD REFER STUDENTS TO THE SARB

To be totally effective, a committee of this nature should be used only when all other avenues of help have been exhausted. Students, as well as parents, should realize that if truancy continues after the SARB meets, the case may be forwarded to juvenile court, which will involve legal action that can take parents away from work and may cost legal fees. Before a student is referred to an attendance review committee, at least three attempts to solve the problem should be documented, together with a record of all truancies and unacceptable absences. (See the section entitled "Administrative Steps to Truancy Control" earlier in this chapter.) Once the three efforts have been made, an administrator or counselor should send a letter informing the parents that their child has been referred to an attendance review board (see Form 1–3) and fill out a referral form (see Form 1–4).

THE SARB'S ROLE IN HELPING TRUANT YOUNGSTERS STAY IN SCHOOL

It is important to remember that the School Attendance Review Board is composed of interested parents, employees of the school, and representatives of other agencies. Their main concern is the welfare of the student. They work cooperatively with probation officers, welfare workers, administrators, teachers, mental health specialists, parents, and community agencies, exploring possible methods of improving student attendance and behavioral patterns. In addition to recommending changes in school programs, they make an effort to enhance the student's mental outlook on school and on life in general, as well as attempt to better the student's self-image. If conditions outside the school seem to be a contributing factor, they suggest alternatives and compromises to promote a better environment.

THE ATTENDANCE COMMITTEE: A HELPING HAND FOR OVERWORKED ADMINISTRATORS

The attendance review board has two main functions:

1. To provide help for the student and for the family with juvenile truancy problems
2. To assist in charting a course of action that will solve the problem

Administrators and counselors can rely on the committee to follow up when other avenues of attendance enforcement on the local level have been exhausted.

When the committee is available to handle student truancy crises, the administrator is freed to address other school issues. Although the school attendance review meeting is not a court hearing, nor designed to mete out punishment, it does have the power to refer truant youngsters to the juvenile authorities if a solution to the truancy problem cannot be reached. When a student is not returned to a school until the truancy problem is resolved, the administration is free to handle other school problems or other truants and does not have to handle the same cases repeatedly.

If the school attendance review board's efforts fail to help, or if its recommendations and suggestions are ignored, and a referral to the juvenile court system seems too drastic a measure to take, one alternative may be to call for a second attendance review meeting with a County Attendance Review Board.

THE COUNTY ATTENDANCE REVIEW BOARD

The County Attendance Review Board (CARB) is similar to the School Attendance Review Board, but its members are drawn from a wider base and have greater authority. Members of CARB participate because it is part of their job description. For example, a retired police officer would volunteer for SARB but an active truant officer would serve on CARB. Members of the CARB board have the authority to invoke demands upon the family without further "due process." These people can legally impose a fine, require family counseling, or other measures that are deemed necessary to encourage a family to return their offspring to the school system.

While SARB provides a consulting service to the family, CARB is a "last resort" effort to acquaint the family with the legal implications of willful truancy. CARB recommendations, although similar to SARB, are more explicit, are based on state law, and do not contain optional choices for the family. Pupils who fail to comply with the recommendations of CARB are guilty of an infraction.

The CARB is utilized when the actions of the SARB have failed and the student still remains truant. When a county attendance review meeting is required, it is recommended that the school administration go through the same process it performed for the initial attendance review meeting: At least two warning letters should be sent to the household, and an administrator of the local school should attempt to schedule a conference by phoning the home.

Should the meeting with the CARB not convince the student to return to regular attendance, the administration has no alternative but to file a petition to juvenile court.

THE STRONG AND WEAK POINTS
OF THE ATTENDANCE REVIEW BOARD SYSTEM

The official actions of the school administrators and the utilization of School Attendance Review Board committees are often enough to rehabilitate a wayward truant. However, the cooperation of the parent is essential in making the program work. Often the parent does not have the influence needed to impress the juvenile with the need for going to school and for obeying the laws that require attendance. A combination of parent and school, working together, has a greater chance than either working separately. Joint efforts result in more successes than failures.

There appear to be some minor weak spots in the system that need shoring up. Too much time is lost between the discovery that the student is a chronic truant and the initiation of authoritative action. The process of taking the first administrative steps, including the initial phone call to the parent and the long wait for the first conference, can be time-consuming. In the event that the parent cannot or will not discipline the juvenile, there is a further delay while the required warning letters are written and delivered. In many cases, by the time this basic procedure is completed the student has been out of school for almost two months. In addition, in overcrowded districts there is usually a waiting period of up to four weeks before the committee can interview the student. During this entire period, the student is out on the street bragging to his peers about how he licked the system. There is no legal way that he can be forced to go to school before the required actions are taken.

It is only at this point, when so much time has been lost, that the juvenile authorities will take over the incorrigibles. In most cases, the authorities will not take action until the student has been through the SARB process. For the most part, juvenile authorities are concerned with acts of crime—and truancy is not a criminal offense. The system needs changes in the education codes that will expedite legal steps that administrators can take to force youth back into the classroom. Above all, it needs more personnel to handle the ever-increasing truancy workload.

PARENTAL REACTIONS TO SCHOOL TRUANCY LAW ENFORCEMENT

Although the parent may feel a growing animosity toward school personnel because they enforce the rules, it should be emphasized that it is the state that mandates the truancy laws. The school district merely administers them.

It is important that administrators explain to parents that school districts are required by law to pursue deviant or truant students and to bring the parents to accountability, using the most effective procedures available. These procedures, which may include parent conferences, written notices, and home visitations, are sometimes perceived by the parent as nothing more than harassment. This is especially true if the parent claims that the child is out of control and that any attempt at parental guidance of discipline would be futile.

WHEN TRUANCY BECOMES A MATTER
FOR THE STATE LAW ENFORCERS

A parent's claim that a youngster is out of control is not considered an adequate excuse for truancy in the eyes of the law, and unless extraordinary conditions exist, no leeway or pardon is granted. Since a person under the age of eighteen usually cannot be tried as an adult (with some exceptions), the parent becomes the individual who is charged under the law. If it becomes apparent that it is beyond the capabilities of the available community services or education programs to change the deviant youngster's behavior—or if the parents fail to follow through on the directives issued by school administrators—then the school district must request that the probation department file a petition on behalf of the minor in juvenile court. The school district also has the option of asking the district attorney to file a complaint against the parents in an effort to force them to control a youngster who is causing recurring problems on campus.

Under the law, it is the parents' responsibility to see that their children attend school until they graduate or until they reach the age when the law allows them to leave. If a student's case is serious enough to warrant arrest and a compulsory court appearance, it is not unusual for the court to impose a fine on the parents.

Education codes in most states contain a statement such as this: "Any parent, guardian, or other person having charge of any pupil who fails to comply with or follow directions from school administrators is guilty of an infraction and shall be punished." This punishment usually consists of any or all of the following: a fine, ranging from $25 to $250; a court-ordered counseling session that must be attended weekly for a period of months or years; or a jail term of five to twenty-five days. These penalties are levied on the parents, not on the youngster.

PARENTS LACK MAGICAL CAPABILITIES AND
HAVE LIMITATIONS

School personnel should always keep in mind that *parents feel confused about dealing with their adolescent children*. The parents' former discipline and control no longer work. Even when things are going moderately well, parents are anxious about their youngster's safety and well-being. Once a child reaches puberty, all the training the child received in the past becomes merely guidance. The child no longer feels forced to respond to the parent's commands, and there is little or nothing the parent can do. At this point, to comply with the further demands of the school district seems like an impossibility to the frustrated parent.

CASE HISTORY OF JOHN: DRUG ABUSE AND TRUANCY

Although he had smoked a few cigarettes, at age thirteen John had never tried marijuana. He excused his cigarette smoking on the theory that both his parents smoked "a couple of packs a day"—and they seemed healthy. Overall, John was a nice boy with good manners and strong ethical standards. He knew the rules laid down by his parents and followed them.

With his solid background, good foundation, and well-adjusted status, it would seem that John's behavioral patterns had been formed permanently. But fate has a way of creating circumstances and occurrences that can shatter the highest ideals and good intentions of even the strongest and most mature individuals, much less those of a youthful and inexperienced teenager.

Upon returning from school one day, John was shocked to learn that the family would be moving to a distant town that was only one-third the size of the one in which they presently resided. However, once accustomed to the idea, John was not greatly opposed to the move. Although he disliked leaving his best friends, he was not antagonistic. Inwardly, he felt that his record of good grades would support him in making a fresh start and gaining a new clique of comrades.

Family Dissension Usually Leads to Bigger Problems

His parents' marriage, however, was unstable, and grew verbally more violent each year. At times, John would come to his mother's defense, but his younger sister always sided with her father. This situation split the family and often turned a parental disagreement into a family dispute that would last for days. In a new town with no friends and such unrest in his family, John felt alienated.

Unknown to his parents, problems at school were just beginning for John. His hope of finding a place with a new circle of friends did not materialize. He became even more lonesome and felt "totally out of it." He existed in a world of solitary isolation.

When John finally did latch on to someone whom he could call a friend, it did not turn out to be a compatible relationship. Rather, it was one of leader and follower. Apparently, John's new "friend" had ulterior motives for becoming involved with John. He was a drug dealer.

Halfway through the school year, John's mannerisms and behavior pattern began to change. He became more and more moody and withdrawn. It was at this stage of John's drug addiction that his parents received a letter requesting their attendance at a school attendance review meeting. John was in the first stages of becoming a high school dropout.

Although his parents did not know it, this letter was not the first the school had sent. John had intercepted and successfully hidden or disposed of a number of prior communications.

The SARB Helps Begin the Healing Process

At the meeting, John's parents sat in shocked silence as they learned the full history of John's poor attendance, failing grades, belligerent behavior on campus, and insubordinate attitude toward his teachers. The young adult that was presented was a complete stranger to them.

In defense of his truancy, John mentioned events and circumstances that neither the administrators nor the parents had known about. His testimony revealed that he had suffered threats of bodily harm from various racial groups and on one occasion was actually mugged. Not having successfully integrated with a clique, he had no protection on campus from their abuse. His solution was to leave school. Absenteeism was less stressful.

His only "friend" had slowly introduced John to drugs that created a state of euphoria within him and relieved his anxiety and his loneliness. Instead of studying in school, he had spent his days learning ways to get money to support his drug habit. He had been introduced to a new way of life.

The SARB's Decision

Considering John's revelations, the committee members and John's parents agreed that it would be academically and emotionally traumatic for John to have to return to a campus he feared. The committee made three strong recommendations:

1. John was to attend a drug rehabilitation center.
2. He was to continue to complete high school credits toward a diploma by studying at home through the district home study program. (More information on this program will be presented in Chapter 12.)
3. He would be returned to comprehensive high school in a few months—after his release from the drug rehabilitation center.

The School's Initiative Results in a Happy Ending

Shortly after the SARB meeting, John moved to a nearby state to reside with an older half-sister until things "cooled off." He attended a drug rehabilitation center where he received excellent counseling that opened up a new outlook on life for him. He then returned to his parents' home and began putting his life back together.

He graduated from a comprehensive high school in the district (other than the one he attended initially) and found a job working full time for a company that taught him marketing skills. He also enrolled at a junior college two nights a week, with the aim of earning an A.A. degree in marketing management.

It is easy to imagine that things might have been different for John if a School Attendance Review Board hadn't been on hand to take action against a developing pattern that would almost surely have led to his dropping out of school.

Today, John is a productive citizen in society, not just another drug addict forced to steal money to support a habit. The first step in John's recovery was the school system's action in recognizing the problem and then initiating immediate remedial steps.

(SCHOOL LETTERHEAD)

_____
(Date)

Dear __(Parent's Name)__ :

    As we have discussed previously, __(student's name)__ continues to have severe attendance problems, primarily an excessive number of unapproved absences. A truant is defined as a student who is absent from school without valid excuse in excess of 30 minutes. A student reported absent ____ times is considered to be a "habitual truant" and is subject to action by the school district.

    The following Education Code laws define a parent's responsibility for sending their child to school.

(Insert education code excerpt here)

    I am aware that you have been dealing with this problem for some time. This letter is to confirm the problem and inform you that we will need to schedule a parent conference in the near future. I am notifying the School District Welfare and Attendance chairman about your child's problem and may request intervention at that level if this pattern continues.

    Please call me at __(phone number)__ to arrange a conference time to discuss this matter further.

Sincerely,

_____
Principal

cc: Chairman, Child Welfare and Attendance
    Student File

Form 1–1

(SCHOOL LETTERHEAD)

_____(Date)_____

Dear _____(Parent's Name)_____:

This letter is to confirm our appointment scheduled for __(date)__ at ___ o'clock to discuss the attendance problem of __(student's name)__. At this conference, we will make every attempt to resolve the reasons for your child's poor attendance.

As you were previously notified, continued nonattendance may result in referral to the School Attendance Review Board and a possible referral to an outside agency. It is my hope that we can discuss the problem and possible solutions together with your child in order to avoid this step.

I would appreciate your close attention to this matter and look forward to meeting with you and your child at the planned time. It is important that we make an effort together to find the cause of your child's truancy and plan possible solutions. Should we be unable to resolve the problem, it will become necessary to refer you and your child to our Attendance Review Board.

Sincerely,

_____

Principal

cc: Chairman, Child Welfare and Attendance
    Student File

Form 1–2

_____ (Date)

Dear ____(Parent's Name)____ :

This letter is to inform you that, because of continued unexcused absences, your child, _(student's name)_ , has been declared a "habitual truant." Therefore, I have submitted his/her name to the School Attendance Review Board for possible intervention at the district level or referral to an outside agency.

The School Attendance Review Board will notify you in the near future of the date, time, and place of the hearing. You will be asked to bring your child with you. At the close of the hearing, you will be given instructions as to his/her school attendance. It is imperative that you schedule time to attend this meeting. A representative from the school will also be in attendance.

If you wish to discuss this matter further, please contact me at _(phone number)_ . I consider this matter to be very important and will assist in any way possible to help your family solve this problem.

Sincerely,

_____

Principal

cc: Chairman, Child Welfare and Attendance
    Student File

REFERRAL TO ATTENDANCE REVIEW BOARD

Name of Referring School _____

Date of Referral _____

Student's Name _____ Grade _____

Age _____ Birth Date _____ Telephone _____

Address _____

_____

Reading Test Scores _____ Math Test Scores _____

Teacher and/or staff contact information _____

_____

_____

_____

Documents attached:

( ) Attendance Report   ( ) Copy of letters sent to home

( ) Grade Report   ( ) Other _____

_____
Signature of Person Making Referral

_____
Title

_____
Phone Number

_____
School

Form 1–4

The Counselor's Part in Recognizing and Redirecting Potential Dropouts

The term "helping relationship" defines the role of the counselor. Counselors endeavor, through interaction with the student, to modify, enrich, and guide their students' behavior so that a positive change results.

In our schools, most demands on counselors are made by psychologically intact adolescents—youngsters who need help only because they face the common developmental stresses of teenage life. These individuals fall into the category of "normal." They conform to the standard or average type. However, in some cases even so-called "normal behavior" may deviate somewhat from acceptable social behavior. Some adolescent developmental stages trigger a need for a youngster to deviate from his or her normal state of being. For instance, a momentary desire to "fit in with the group" may result in an act of showing off by back talking a teacher, vandalism, or cutting class. Although "show off" is a normal behavior for adolescents, the deviant acts are considered abnormal. A counselor would help the youngsters redirect this "acting out" into a more acceptable form such as participating in a wrestling club, drama class, or after school sports.

When a student does appear to abrogate the code, she or he will most likely be categorized as "abnormal" and in need of counseling help. The student will then be referred to a more highly specialized professional, such as a clinical psychologist.

THE FIRST STEP IN THE PROCESS OF DROPOUT PREVENTION

It is important to note that in most cases the initial referral of a student to a counselor is made by one of the teenager's teachers.

Teachers are a vital link in the recognition of distress among students and are the chief instigators in seeing that help is eventually given to a troubled youth. Teacher observations play such a major part in diagnosing and controlling deviant behavior that it is not surprising to find that the largest percentage of referrals to counseling come from alert and perceptive classroom educators. Some of the symptoms that teachers have learned to recognize as indications of potential dropout are:

1. Change of attitude
2. Falling grades
3. Change in work or dress habits
4. Excessive tardiness or absence

Once a teacher is alerted to any one of, or any combination of, these changes, the teacher dispatches a referral memorandum to the counselor. The counselor responds by confronting the youngster with his or her unacceptable behavior. This initial meeting is principally diagnostic in nature and the problem may be solved immediately through a simple solution. On the other hand, it may become apparent that the student needs extended assistance. In cases such as these, the counselor must be prepared to approach the problem on a proven professional basis.

The Meeting Place Can Set the Ambience for Success or Failure

When a confrontation with a pupil is planned, the site of the meeting must be chosen wisely. A proper atmosphere can be an asset, and is often instrumental in setting the stage for an accurate and speedy resolution.

It is a good idea to avoid using the principal's office, chiefly because of the negative connotation the students attach to it as a place of punishment. Such a location could cast a psychological pall over the meeting.

A better place would be the counselor's office, but it, too, is usually humming with routine business and is often located in a highly active area where the student is exposed to distracting outside influences, lessening the tranquility that is needed to establish productive rapport.

Experience has shown that the best place is some neutral territory where the student can feel unhampered. Strangely enough, these locations are such places as:

1. The facility room or a neutral alternative classroom with which the student is familiar

2. The nurse's office

3. Outside the school building on a bench or under a tree

4. In any empty classroom where there is no risk of interruption

The young person will be less inhibited and more apt to respond to tactful questions if he or she feels comfortable with the surroundings and the meeting takes place in a nonthreatening environment.

WHO SHOULD ATTEND THE DIAGNOSTIC MEETING

Along with the counselor and the troubled young person, other participants who can be included for their input contribution and/or professional expertise are the teacher (or other party) who referred the student, the parent or guardian, and the troubled youngster's best friend.

In a case where the referring party is a teacher she or he can supply important details about the student's behavior, compare past and present grade performance, offer observations on personality traits and attitudes, and vouch for any changes in the student's general physical appearance. The teacher's close daily relationship and familiarity with the troubled youth are helpful in setting right any erroneous or unclear answers the youngster might inadvertently make.

If a parent or guardian attends the meeting, she or he would be able to supply accurate information about family background and history. Often, however, the presence of a parental figure can cause the young person to "clam up," depending on the circumstances and the closeness of the relationship. For this reason, some consideration should be given to conducting at least a portion of the meeting without the parental authority figure present.

Some counselors feel that inviting a best friend will complicate matters. In many cases, however, close friends can be instrumental in speeding up the diagnostic process because of their intimate knowledge about the student and his or her affairs. In a nonthreatening situation, a close friend is usually willing to talk about such things as:

1. Family "closet secrets" (these often shed light on the basic reasons behind the sudden change in classroom behavior)

2. The troubled youth's home situation and living environment

3. The personal routine and habits of his or her good friend with relation to sleeping, eating, and studying

The "close friend" also often provides a crutch for his or her troubled buddy, making it easier for the youngster to answer questions that he or she may be reluctant to talk to anybody else about. Clandestine, heads-down, huddled conversations often provide more answers than almost any other part of the meeting. Allowing long pauses between questions, permitting the youngster an opportunity to collect his or her thoughts, and listening carefully are practices that tend to maintain a nonthreatening atmosphere that encourages free-flowing expression. Although a particular response may not be pertinent to the question asked, it is a good idea to allow the student to talk uninterruptedly. Any attempt to insist that answers be strictly congruent will be a "turn-off." It is most important to let the troubled youth talk once he or she starts. Unanswered questions can always be interposed at a more suitable time.

HOW COUNSELORS EMPLOY THE PERSONAL TOUCH TO HELP STUDENTS SOLVE THEIR OWN PROBLEMS

Teenagers usually drop out because they develop physical or emotional traumas that make it impossible for them to cope with the stresses of life. These problems stem from, but are not limited to, such things as:

1. A bad or intolerable home situation
2. Conflict with peers on campus
3. Conflict with teachers
4. Undiagnosed learning needs
5. Physical handicaps or mental retardation

Once problems surface, the teacher may seek to help the student through referral to counseling.

With parental permission, the counselor can meet with the family once or twice weekly in private session, or with the student alone. Should a counselor feel that no progress is being made, usually because of a personality conflict, the student—along with other members of the family, if they are being counseled—should be transferred to a more compatible counselor within the school district or the community.

MAKING USE OF COMMUNITY SERVICES THAT PROVIDE ADDED HELP

A good working tool for counselors to possess is a ready list of community aid services. When additional help is needed, help that is beyond the capacity of the counselor to give independently, it is important to be able to name an appropriate organization or institution and give a complete description of the services it offers. The address, telephone number, and name of the person in charge are essential. Such a list might differ from state to state and county to county, but the following rundown will serve as a guideline for making up a list for your district:

1. Substance abuse prevention programs
2. Community counseling services
3. Children and adult protective services
4. Employment opportunity options
5. Planned Parenthood center
6. General county health services
7. Crime victims resource center
8. District alternative education programs
9. Community legal services
10. Welfare and social services

The community mental health service is an excellent establishment to which to refer troubled youngsters and their families, although extreme discretion should be used when making the referral. It provides a setting where those who work in the counseling profession can gather and serve the community jointly. Many professionals in community counseling also hold positions as high school counselors, social workers, or probation officers. Mental health services are usually available to the public at a nominal cost or for a fee commensurate with the patient's or family's income level. Generally, fees are predicated on the gross income of the patient. Families falling within established low-income parameters are counseled free of charge.

OTHER AREAS OF AVAILABLE HELP WITH WHICH COUNSELORS SHOULD BE FAMILIAR

Some communities and areas have local camps where juvenile offenders can be committed—usually through court order—for specific periods of time. These are not recreation camps, but places where youngsters receive discipline, schooling, and redirection. Parents are normally charged a monthly rate for the care of their offspring at these places.

There are also private agencies that provide free counseling services by volunteer workers and professionals. These agencies are generally funded by donations from the city and from private philanthropy. Persons who staff these agencies are dedicated individuals who are imbued with a deep desire to help humanity and especially the growing teenager seeking maturity.

These agencies provide food and lodging for runaways and are a source of medical help for drug abusers.

Counselors or individuals who would like more detailed information on these agencies can write or call the county education offices, the chamber of commerce, or the state department of social services and welfare. These are generally listed in the white pages of the telephone directory under the state, county, or local government listings. Counselors who are resourceful in accumulating this kind of information will not only find it greatly helpful in the performance of their own duties, but can render a service by passing it along to other teachers and parents for their use.

Another important community service that contributes to dropout prevention is the teen hotline.

To have a fully functional system, it is essential that when teenagers make use of the service, they feel confident that they will not be subjected to reprimands, recriminations, or lectures, and that no attempt will be made to trace the call or to apprehend the caller. Failure to adhere to these vital requirements will negate any usefulness the hotline might have, simply because youngsters will not respond once the word is out. It is also foremost in importance that callers understand that only requested information, such as referrals to available lodging, counseling, protection, and medical assistance, will be dispensed. Under no circumstances should pressure ever be applied to get callers to reveal their location, and law enforcement agents must never be notified unless it is determined that the caller is involved in a life-threatening situation. The only deviation from the standard of complete anonymity is when the caller is a runaway. Then the hotline operator may appeal to the caller to supply a family phone number so that parents or guardians can be notified of the runaway's well-being and health status.

A critical factor in the development of a counselor's knowledge and expertise is the cultivation of close professional relationships with local police officers, drug counselors, camp directors, park and recreational leaders, and other providers of youth services in the community. These persons are often the connecting link in locating absent students, assisting them in solving their problems, and returning them to the educational system.

LEARNING STYLES: A DIAGNOSTIC TOOL USED BY COUNSELORS FOR RETURNING DROPOUTS TO THE EDUCATIONAL SYSTEM

In general, schools operate on the assumptions that young people learn the same way and that they function best between the hours of 8:00 A.M. and 5:00 P.M.—notions that have existed in educational theory since the eighteenth century. There is a tendency among many people to look upon those who do not perform well during standard business hours as having a character flaw, or maybe an affliction. They are often labeled *lazy, incorrigible, truant, learning-handicapped, juvenile delinquent,* or *potential dropout.*

However, it has become more and more evident that there are dramatic differences in functional capabilities among individuals. Differences abound in conceptualization, perception, and comprehension. These variations are inherent in each person's learning style as well. Some people learn best by the audio process (hearing), others through visual conception (seeing), while still others absorb information best through a kinesthetic (sensorimotor) experience. Some people learn better in the morning hours, while others do not approach alertness until midday.

The fact is that people cannot alter their innate learning style, no matter how much, or in what manner, convention may require them to do so.

How Diagnosing Learning Styles in Underachievers Helps Curb Truancy and Prevents Dropout

A school district in California designated two control groups of under-achievers and assessed their learning styles. The results showed that 80 percent of these youngsters tended to be *post meridiem* learners, or afternoon learners. The students scored higher on achievement tests when the tests were administered in the afternoon hours rather than in the morning hours.

The first control group consisted mostly of chronically truant youngsters who tended to miss the first and second periods of the day. For the sake of the study analyses, this group was allowed to start its school day at 11:00 A.M. and attend until 3:00 P.M.

Under these conditions, the truancy rate for the first group dropped by 75 percent, and the grades of the participants improved dramatically.

The second control group consisted mainly of habitual underachievers. This group took elective classes in the morning hours and mandatory academic classes after 11:00 A.M. The truancy rate for this group remained almost constant, showing little or no improvement, but the students' grade point averages in academic subjects, such as reading, writing, and math showed a remarkable increase.

Proper assessment and scheduling of youngsters who seem to learn better in the afternoon hours is a counselor's and administrator's nightmare. Most schools are already so overcrowded, and the popular classes so full, that it is nearly impossible to plan afternoon openings for a specific group of students. The answer generally lies in making use of alternative programs such as continuation high school (see Chapter 3), independent study (see Chapter 4), vocational training (see Chapters 5 and 6), and other special services. These programs are specifically implemented with the potential dropout in mind and offer a variety of class times.

When Alternative Programs Are Not Available to *Post Meridiem* Learners

Although teachers should be sensitive to how their pupils learn, it is even more important to ensure that each student understands his or her own inherent and genetically determined learning style. This allows the student to realize that there is nothing basically wrong with his or her ability to learn and gives the student a measure of conscious control over the learning process, thus raising confidence and generating motivation.

A student in a comprehensive high school who has undergone a learning style assessment analysis and who has seen the results can assist a counselor to construct an appropriate class schedule. Counselor and student can, for instance, make an effort to enroll the *ante meridiem*, or morning, learner in first- and second-period academic classes and hold open the P.M. academic classes for afternoon learners. Study hall and other elective courses can be used to fill in any gaps in the schedule.

HOW SPECIALIZED PERSONNEL TEAMS HELP IN RETRIEVING DROPOUTS

When a student is referred to specialized personnel by the teacher, counselor, or administrator, prior to any remedial action, it is imperative that the child be properly diagnosed. It has been demonstrated that delinquent youngsters who seem unable to follow rules can sometimes be misdiagnosed and labeled retarded when the real problem may be purely emotional.

In an effort to be as certain as possible that a student is properly diagnosed, most districts have developed a child study team. This team is usually made up of one or more qualified teachers, counselors, and at least one staff psychologist employed by the school, together with a resource specialist and a speech therapist. The objective of this team of specialized personnel is to evaluate the youngster and to arrive at a joint understanding of the reasons for the youngster's delinquency or deviant behavior.

HOW A DIAGNOSTIC EVALUATION FOR SPECIAL EDUCATION IS MADE

Some students may drop out simply because the work is too hard for them. Many times, these are young people with a learning handicap who need to be placed in a proper setting in order to give them an equal opportunity to learn. Some types of mental retardation, such as Down's syndrome, are apparent from birth. Hypothyroidism and hydrocephaly are examples of diseases that produce mental retardation and that may not become apparent until shortly after birth or within the first few months or years. Family and friends become accustomed to the child's less-than-normal functioning, and he or she is accepted as being merely "a little slow" or "not too bright."

Generally, youngsters with a mental disability that is diagnosed early do not need an evaluation by the child study team. The study team is concerned mostly with cases of mild mental retardation in children who have no previous history of brain pathology. This type of child frequently reaches the upper elementary grades without anyone suspecting that she or he has a mental deficiency, though in school, just as in the home, the child may be labeled *slow, disruptive,* or even *bad.*

In the course of making the evaluation, the team usually follows guidelines such as these:

1. The parent is notified and permission to proceed is requested.
2. The student's present teacher submits a preassessment summary that includes the child's:
   a. Test scores
   b. Attendance records
   c. Apparent health condition
   d. Classroom behavior evaluation
   e. Academic skills evaluation
3. A learning problems profile is submitted by the teacher. (See Form 2–1.)
4. Current samples of the student's academic work in spelling, reading, math, and language are appraised.
5. The cumulative folder is examined for contributing content. (The cumulative folder is a complete history of the child's activities and progress while in school. It includes grades, health records, exam results, referrals, etc.)
6. The child is interviewed, tested, and given a physical examination.

Upon completion of the six preceding steps, the child study team will choose one of the following options:

1. The pupil may remain in the regular class, with provision made for special material, special equipment, additional consultation, and/or additional assistance by the teacher.
2. The pupil may be enrolled in the regular program and receive special support services, which can include adapted physical education, speech or language therapy, counseling, and specific assistance for impairments of hearing or vision.

3. The pupil may be enrolled in the regular program for the majority of the school day and receive assistance from a resource specialist.

4. The pupil may be enrolled in a special education class for the majority of the school day. The class will provide instructional emphasis for the student's special needs.

5. The pupil may be enrolled in a private school if the special services appropriate for the student's needs are not available in the regular public school program.

Special Education Classes: What They Consist of and How They Help Prevent Dropout

Special education classes led by specially trained teachers are designed to serve students with mental or physical handicaps.

The curriculum for mild retardates concentrates on basic social skills, money management, and simple occupational skills. In addition, some academic subjects, such as reading and math, are also taught.

Experience has proven that students who attend these classes learn to function better at home and are more likely to become productive members of society. Aside from the humanitarian value of providing the mentally retarded with appropriate training and education, it benefits society in general, since the cost of lifetime institutionalization is very high. The acquisition of vocational skills enables the retarded person to become more independent and to escape becoming another tax-supported burden on the community.

Since there is seldom a need to adjust or rearrange mandatory academic subjects for the physically handicapped, the curriculum for these students replicates that of the traditional high school. It also includes physical therapy and specialized help in any area deemed necessary, such as speech therapy for the deaf, braille books for the blind, and the help of an assistant to empty catheter bags and push a wheelchair, along with any other training that may be needed to sustain daily survival.

One of the more common services is psychological counseling. This is especially helpful to the physically handicapped, who often must deal with feelings of inferiority, self-pity, fear, and hostility. These emotional conflicts are especially prominent during adolescence, when physical appearance plays so important a part in attaining peer-group status. Overt defects can be highly stressful to a teenager.

How Special Education Schools Are Funded

Special education schools are funded principally by state legislative grants and monies based on ADA (average daily attendance). Getting funds through ADA is usually a complicated process that requires a written report on each child, setting forth the degree of handicap, the psychological and physical services that must be rendered, and the frequency of attendance. This procedure takes precious time away from the qualified personnel who dedicate their lives and energy to helping the handicapped.

Why It Is Essential for Some Handicapped Students to Attend Special Classes

Approximately 70 percent of handicapped youngsters attend school on a traditional campus. This applies especially to the physically handicapped, including the blind, the hard of hearing, and those confined to wheelchairs. Arrangements are made so that competent help is available to these young people when any personal needs arise that they cannot handle on their own while on campus.

In the case of the borderline retarded student, the teacher in regular school can adapt a program of study on an appropriate level to accommodate the child. This solution works well when one pupil meets with one teacher for most of the day. However, at the high school level, where students move from teacher to teacher, borderline retardates often have difficulty adjusting and may be placed in special education classes.

Special Education as a Dropout Prevention Program

Many educators fail to see the value of special education as a dropout prevention implement. However, when a young deviate causes havoc in a classroom, learning ceases for everyone there. If, on the other hand, a diagnostic evaluation has shown that the youngster would be better off in a special education class, and the deviant youngster is placed in an environment where she or he can succeed, the prevention system is functioning. It seems reasonable to assume that if special education classes halt that young person's mounting frustrations, the potential for eventual dropout has been removed.

CASE HISTORY OF KARLA: A POTENTIAL DROPOUT

There was nothing about Karla that made her stand out in a crowd. She was of average height and weight, with brown eyes, straight hair, and a generally mediocre appearance. She had already been labeled a "square peg" by her peers and did nothing to discourage that appraisal when she joined the dull group that always stood in a secluded corner at dances and other student activities.

No one in the system had an inkling that Karla was, in reality, a deeply troubled young lady with severe problems at home. It was only a very sudden drop in grades and a drastic change in attitude that finally focused the school personnel's attention on her. It was Karla's English teacher who actually issued the written referral to Karla's counselor.

How the Counselor Made Use of an
Outside Agency to Help Karla

In an interview with Karla, the counselor was at first unable to pinpoint a reasonable explanation for Karla's sudden behavior change. A stalemate was created by her repetitive "I don't know" responses to direct questions. The customary phone call to the parent produced nothing but indifference. The mother refused to attend a conference with the counselor and there was no biological father in the home.

Karla's deportment changes continued to accelerate, and within a week of her initial interview, she was cited with three more behavior referrals. This made it even more evident that Karla desperately needed help. Despite Karla's uncooperative attitude, the referral counselor felt that there was help for Karla among one of the resource agencies, if she could choose the right one. As an alternative to the unsuccessful therapy she was already giving, the counselor suggested to Karla that she make use of the Crisis Center. With Karla's permission, she personally drove her there and escorted her inside.

The atmosphere at the new setting seemed to have a salving effect on Karla's inner turmoil. It became immediately obvious that she was more relaxed. She was introduced to an on-duty community counselor who scheduled regular sessions. These produced an outpouring of pent-up emotions that brought the problem to the surface.

The Suppressed Emotional Problem that
Triggered the Behavior Changes

Karla's problem had its roots in the death of her father, a tragedy that occurred when she was nine years old. His death not only had its initial impact on Karla, but it left her mother financially troubled and emotionally devastated. She turned to liquor for solace. Within six months she was a full-blown alcoholic.

Karla's older brother, who was a sophomore in college, provided the only stability in her life. She leaned heavily on him for support, the two of them forming a coalition for survival that included forging their mother's signature on her welfare checks so they could pay the bills and perform the other adult responsibilities of running the home. For all practical purposes, the roles in the household had switched and the children were nurturing the parent.

Although Karla's brother proved to be an excellent mentor, she missed the emotional tie to her parents. She had been close to her own father, and this gap in her life remained unfulfilled. There was little love or reassurance to be gleaned from her mother, who was seldom coherent.

The situation disintegrated completely when her mother introduced a friend into the home as her live-in boyfriend. He was a hulking heavyweight who was well set in his own alcoholic ways. Although he was kind and gentle when sober, his drinking triggered violence and frightening sexual deviation patterns in his conduct. He often struck Karla's mother, and then turned on Karla when she tried to defend her mother. Night after night, he raped Karla while she screamed in terror and her mother and brother stood by helplessly.

In desperation, her mother remained sober long enough to notify the police and file battery, rape, and trespass charges against him. But the action only backfired. Within twenty-four hours bail was arranged and the arrested rapist was released to prey on his victims again.

In the interim, Karla's brother reached the age of twenty and, unable to tolerate the environment any longer, he moved out. Karla fell apart completely. With her last refuge gone, she felt totally alone and rejected. Her interest in a better life disappeared and her repressed troubles manifested themselves outwardly in her behavior at school. She was well on her way to becoming a high school dropout.

How School Counselors Collaborate With Community Services to Prevent Dropout

Once the facts about Karla's life were brought to light, her counselor notified the authorities. The Social Services department dispatched a worker who investigated conditions in the home and arranged for Karla to attend group counseling sessions for teenagers with alcoholic parents. It took a week to verify the reasons for removing Karla from her home environment and then she was placed in a suitable foster home.

To be permitted to stay in her foster home, Karla had to meet certain criteria and agree to precise contractual stipulations. She was required to

1. Attend community counseling sessions twice a week
2. Check in briefly once a week with her school counselor
3. Stay in school (not drop out)

Epilogue

Fortunately, Karla was astute enough to envision the benefits of the counseling sessions and to understand and willingly accept the help she needed to cope with the emotional turmoil brought on by her mother's live-in friend.

She maintains a feeling of gratitude toward the school personnel and realizes they were all of tremendous help to her. She did not run away, turn to crime, become a drug addict, or drop out of school. She graduated from high school and went on to become a mature, productive, and self-supporting citizen.

In the final analysis, Karla stayed in school because her personal problems were solved through the efforts and planning of the district's dropout prevention program.

LEARNING PROBLEMS PROFILE CHECKLIST

In many cases, children display behavior patterns that impede their ability to learn. They alert teachers and parents that such a condition may exist.

Classroom Behavior

[ ] Moves constantly
[ ] Has difficulty beginning or completing tasks
[ ] Is often tardy or absent
[ ] Is generally quiet or withdrawn
[ ] Is disorganized
[ ] Has difficulty with peer relationships
[ ] Is easily distracted by sights or sounds
[ ] Displays inconsistencies in behavior
[ ] Seems to misunderstand oral directions
[ ] May do the same thing again and have difficulty shifting to a new activity, or stopping when it is time
[ ] May not know what day of the week it is, or the time of day, the month, or the year
[ ] May not seem to remember something previously learned
[ ] May appear to be bright but does not seem to be learning to read, spell, or do arithmetic
[ ] May be erratic in his or her performance
[ ] May feel personally frustrated, or stupid, and may see herself or himself as a failure

Academic Symptoms

Reading:

[ ] Loses place, repeats words
[ ] Does not read fluently
[ ] Confuses similar words and letters
[ ] Uses finger to follow along
[ ] Subvocalizes when reading
[ ] Does not read willingly
[ ] Does not look at the whole word when reading

Arithmetic:

[ ] Has difficulty associating number with symbol
[ ] Cannot remember math facts
[ ] Fails to note process signs
[ ] Confuses columns and spaces
[ ] Has difficulty with story problems
[ ] Fails to comprehend math concepts

Spelling:

[ ] Uses incorrect order of letters in words
[ ] Has difficulty associating correct sound with appropriate letter
[ ] Reverses letters and words (mirror imagery)

Writing:

[ ] Cannot stay on line
[ ] Has difficulty copying from board or other source
[ ] Use poor written expression for age
[ ] Is slow in completing written work
[ ] Uses cursive writing and printing in same assignment
[ ] Mixes lower and upper case letters in the same word

Verbal Communication:

[ ] Hesitates often when speaking
[ ] Uses poor verbal expression for age
[ ] Inappropriate speaking voice

Motor Responses

[ ] Displays poor coordination
[ ] Has problems of balance
[ ] Confuses right and left
[ ] Cannot consistently cross midline of the body
[ ] Lacks rhythm in movements, loses sequence
[ ] Has poor muscle strength for age

Form 2–1

Continuation Schools: Understanding Alternative Education

Nationwide, public school systems are concerned about adjusting educational programs and personnel in order to balance budgets and still meet the needs of today's students. There is an increasing conviction that a crisis in the administration of public education is developing. The need for change is obvious, but there is great difficulty in getting society as a whole to accept this fact.

Today's curriculum, for instance, is usually a residue of past traditions, when realistically the course of study should encompass science and computer literacy, together with vocational courses in electronics, computer operation, industrial arts, and machining.

There are schoolchildren struggling to memorize foreign language declensions, decipher novels that are of little interest to them, and master mathematical problems that are useless to them once they are out of school. Many youngsters cannot see the relevance their curriculum bears to their lives. They are frustrated by the intuition that they need more up-to-date knowledge that will help them cope with a rapidly changing technological society.

Many bright youngsters tend to drop out of the school system because of the system's reluctance to break with ingrained, traditional methods, curricula, and procedures that they are convinced are no longer germane.

RESISTANCE TO CHANGE OFTEN RESTS
WITH FINANCIAL DILEMMA

Frequently, little opportuntity for program experimentation is available to those schools interested in creating new approaches. Inappropriate allocation of funds or resources hampers creativity. Often the perceptions that community people hold regarding traditional education work against progressive change. For example, bond propositions for the construction of new buildings that could house alternative schools seldom get passed.

Fortunately, there are workable programs for dropout prevention and retrieval that do not demand excessive funding or the presence of experts. These approaches involve the establishment of continuing or alternative education facilities and programs, some of which have been functioning in some states since the 1960s. Unfortunately, however, very few of the progressive and productive advances made in these basically experimental schools have found their way into traditional public schools.

To clarify the term, "alternative school" means a school that is *deliberately* differentiated from other schools in order to accommodate the needs and interests of students who are having trouble in a traditional setting. Such a school is designed to place a special emphasis on the development of close relationships among students and faculty and fosters a sense of belonging. In such an environment, student participation is more individualized. Youngsters are more likely to learn by doing rather than through theoretical oral instruction.

There are various formats for creating alternative schools, including:

1.   Using "open" or "structured" methods
2.   Establishing a separate school
3.   Establishing a satellite school
4.   Creating a school within a school
5.   Through community partnership

CONTINUATION SCHOOLS ARE A SUCCESSFUL ALTERNATIVE

Intrinsically, a continuation school is an alternative school that offers classes consistent with the district's regular course of study. It is defined as a school (or class grouping within a school) that maintains a learning situation geared to maximize student motivation. It encourages youngsters to follow their own interests on a level and through a learning process that produce success. In a continuation school, the district enables the minimum standards for academic achievement and the required curriculum guidelines plus the minimum standards for graduation.

The goals of a continuation school are

1. To provide personalized instruction for each student
2. To provide guidance and counseling services to enhance student self-image
3. To improve communication between parent, child, and school by providing frequent opportunities for interaction between parents and staff
4. To maintain a close liaison between the comprehensive school and the continuation school
5. To provide an opportunity for students to meet the district diploma requirements for graduation
6. To encourage the development of character, including standards of right and wrong
7. To teach moral education, encompassing honesty, integrity, and persistence in the face of adversity
8. To provide a minimum school day for students who must work because of family financial need

Legislation That Provides for Continuation Schools

Legislation for continuation schools generally falls under the category of "special programs in education." The education code will, as a rule, authorize a governing board to establish and maintain within its boundaries special continuation schools or classes. The code will outline legislative intent for all the policies and procedures involved, including referral, attendance, and preparation of courses.

Most states provide reference materials that explain laws relating to minors. These materials generally contain information about the types of alternative education that are legally available in your state. To obtain this and other pertinent materials, call your state department of education.

FUNDING

Generally, state and local funds are allocated to continuation schools in the same manner as to comprehensive schools. The education code referring to the allocation of financial apportionments will explain the distribution of funds. Should the continuation school be located on the same site as a comprehensive school, the allocation must be distributed by the principal within the limits of the local school budget. Should the continuation school be located on a separate site, the program would fall into the category of alternative education and be funded as such. In the unlikely event that there is no legislation regarding alternative education in your state, consult Chapter 13 for the steps a school district may take to begin procedures to obtain such legislation.

OPTIONS IN HOUSING THE CONTINUATION SCHOOL

Continuation schools can be adapted to fit the needs of the district and vary greatly in size. Some are contained within their own campuses and may house 250 to 300 students. Many of these schools have enough space to offer—in addition to the academic curriculum—wood-shop classes, home economics labs in cooking and sewing, art workshops, and computer science courses. Frequently, these schools are located in renovated campuses that were once closed because of decreasing enrollment. Other schools of this sort have been successfully situated within a grouping of portable buildings.

Sometimes continuation schools share a campus with a comprehensive school as a "school within a school," or a row of classrooms may be designated as continuation classrooms. Youngsters who are referred to continuation attend all their classes within these few rooms. Although this setting works for youths who are attending continuation because of personal needs, it may not work well for incorrigible youths who were referred to continuation because of misbehavior. It does, however, relieve a budget problem by alleviating the need to hire additional administrative staff.

Important factors to consider when choosing a continuation school site are:

1.   The population that will be served
2.   Availability of funding
3.   The utilization of school property that is presently sitting idle
4.   Access to portable housing
5.   The ability of the school district to provide transportation to the site
6.   Staffing requirements, such as the availability of a principal, counselor, and clerical aides

WHO ATTENDS CONTINUATION SCHOOLS?

It is not uncommon for a few young people to spend their educational careers leaping from one school to another, never satisfied with the curriculum and constantly blaming the instructors for their own failures. Typically, these students have a long list of excuses for their lack of achievement. Topmost among these is the lack of encouragement and support at home.

Scrutiny of the records usually reveals that these students frequently do not participate as extensively as their peers in the general and social activities of campus life. Generally, they cultivate few friends and almost never engage in extracurricular activities such as sports, the debate team, clubs, and so on.

They are usually poor readers who tried to catch up with special help during their late elementary years—once they began to visualize their entrance into high school. Stigmatized because they needed special help, they are often suffocated by feelings of shame and inferiority. In all likelihood, they never stayed in one school or program long enough to benefit from the effects of simple endurance.

These students usually feel ever-increasing social pressures, as well as personal and economic tensions. They generally fall into one of the following categories:

1. Student is a member of a one-parent family

2. Student comes from a family in which some members are chemically dependent

3. Student has no one in charge of her or him at home

4. Student belongs to a family that moves frequently

5. Student belongs to family in which the person in authority considers school to be a low priority

6. Student or family member has been on probation or has served a short jail sentence

7. Student is not involved in community or school activities

Students with parents who provide poor role models are frequently rebellious and lack respect for authority. Their deficient social training stems from the home environment, where they have few or no restrictions or rules. Because of their inability to deal with the rules and regulations set forth by authority figures in traditional schools, these students thrive in continuation school settings where rules and regulations are designed to meet the needs of these people.

THE REFERRAL PROCESS

In general practice, the governing board of each high school formulates and adopts rules and regulations governing the transfer of referred students to a continuation school. The procedure usually includes:

1. A written notice to the pupil and the pupil's parent or guardian, informing each of the specific reasons for the transfer and giving them an opportunity to request a conference

2. A conference with the pupil and the pupil's parent or guardian in which the reasons for the transfer are discussed and all documents inspected

3. A written statement of the facts and reasons for the transfer, indicating whether the decision is subject to periodic review

4. A completed referral form that gives general information on the student, including date of transfer, address, birth date, parent's name and address, and reasons for transfer (see Form 3–4).

It should be made clear that a student may transfer voluntarily to a continuation school in order to receive individualized instruction or because of personal need. An involuntary transfer is imposed only when other means fail to bring about improvement in the student's academic or social behavior at school. Youngsters who transfer, voluntarily or involuntarily, to continuation school should have the option of transferring back to a regular high school at the beginning of a school year or semester. It is wise to establish criteria for pupils who seek to be reinstated into the traditional setting. These may include

1. Regular attendance (specify the number of days the student may reasonably miss)

2. The minimum number of credits to be acquired by the student while in attendance at continuation school

3. A specific behavior code that must be adhered to

4. Any other requirements set up by the governing board

CURRICULUM IN THE CONTINUATION SCHOOL

Through alternative methods not found in the comprehensive program, continuation school generally provides an education for students who are motivated to complete the units needed for a high school diploma. For this reason, it is important that the curriculum remain consistent with district guideline requirements for graduation. Nonetheless, variations in the method of delivery, size of the classroom, and length of school day are normal. Instructors in continuation schools usually follow these practical guidelines:

1. Set short daily goals

2. Use instructional television and video cassette recorders; include programs that use laser disc players such as the IBM PALS reading program for remediation and ESL classes

3. Develop a class in peer counseling

4. Devote some time to the development of study skills

5. Provide a class in vocational counseling that teaches job-seeking skills and good work habits

6. Offer credit for a class on self-worth and provide easy access to professional counselors

7. It is also advisable to offer remedial classes in language, reading, and math for students with below-average academic skills.

WORK EXPERIENCE: AN INTEGRAL PART
OF CONTINUATION SCHOOLS

Continuation schools are an excellent alternative for youngsters who are at risk of dropping out because they need to work. According to a report issued by the California department of finance, the first continuation schools were established in 1919 to serve young people who had left full-time programs to seek employment.

Typically, the school requires attendance for a minimum of fifteen hours per week (an average of three hours per day), then the student is excused allowing time for the pursuance of outside employment. It is not uncommon for continuation schools to run two shifts, a three-hour section in the morning and another in the afternoon. This flexible schedule allows students to work either a morning or an afternoon job and provides a six-hour teaching day for contracted staff. Students attending a three-hour school day make fewer credits toward graduation than traditional students. The work experience class provides an opportunity for continuation pupils to receive credit equivalent to one or two instructional periods per week. Outside work experience (OWE) class allows high school credit to students who work at paying jobs. Volunteer work in the community, at a school, or as an apprentice is called inside work experience (IWE) and also qualifies for the instructional credit.

Students who receive full credit are generally required to complete "learning aid packets for students" (LAPS) for maximum educational benefit.

Definition of a Work Experience Class

The governing board of any school district, under state and federal law, can provide an optional work experience program that allows students to work in jobs in- or outside the school district. It includes employing pupils in appropriate part-time jobs that have been designated as educational for students, under the supervision of a coordinator who is employed by the school or district. It is recommended that youngsters under the age of eighteen are issued work permits and enrolled in work experience education class. State labor laws vary on the issuance of work permits. It is the responsibility of school district personnel to have a working knowledge of the labor laws in their state. The supervising coordinator

1. Provides one hour a week of classroom instruction in skills necessary for success in employment
2. Provides guidance and supervision that ensure that the student is placed in a suitable job
3. Approves and awards appropriate credit for the work experience class
4. Documents a plan of training, student hours on the job, class time, and any other areas mandated by board or district policy (see Forms 3–1, 3–2, and 3–3)

STAFFING THE CONTINUATION SCHOOL

Generally, instructors who function well in the traditional classroom are successful in the continuation classroom. Although the youngsters are somewhat at risk for dropping out, most have made the decision to stay in school. Any professional services they may require are handled by outside sources.

As is true in any dropout retrieval or prevention program, the staff members should be people who volunteer to teach in alternative education and have some background in dealing with troubled youths. Teachers who excel at teaching college-bound students would most likely be frustrated in the continuation school setting.

WHAT MAKES CONTINUATION SCHOOLS WORK SO WELL AS A DROPOUT PREVENTION PROGRAM?

Continuation school fills a need by providing a school of choice for students with exceptional personal needs. It offers a program of individualized instruction while helping students to fulfill their compulsory education requirements, and it provides a short school day for youngsters who must work to support families.

Studies have shown that students feel an increased desire to stay in school when rapport with teachers is successfully established. Because continuation schools are structured for greater flexibility and offer activities that are specifically designed to encourage active student participation, there is a greater opportunity to establish a beneficial rapport among students and staff. Combining a motivational curriculum, small classes, an ongoing remedial academic program, with the option of a work experience education class, produces a successful dropout prevention program.

SOCIETAL CHANGE MAKES ALTERNATIVE EDUCATION
A VIABLE OPTION

The attrition rate for school-age youngsters has grown steadily for all races and ethnicities and in all geographic areas. Much of this is due to societal change: the breakup of the nuclear family and the change in moral values.

How do youngsters affected adversely by these changes fit into the educational system? The answer lies in alternative education. Continuation schools provide an educational environment that meets the needs of a generation confronted with unprecedented problems. Some of these problems include

1.   Stress: Achievement-oriented students feel pressure to succeed, be popular, and get good grades, but are not prepared for failure. They may avoid school rather than face a challenge—say, a written test—that they feel they cannot pass. Although parents are a factor, students frequently put undue academic pressure on themselves.

2.   Flawed Parental Role Model: Youngsters who are given no parental guidelines, or whose parents are drug abusers or law breakers, are likely to drop out of school in favor of other, more attractive pastimes. Because education is a low priority of the parent, the child feels free to leave school.

3.   Pregnancy: Each year more than a million teenagers become pregnant. Only half of those who give birth before age eighteen ever complete high school. Many girls elect to keep their babies and raise them outside marriage. They simply have no time for school.

4.   Family Dissension: When parents get divorced, it is often the child who suffers most. Teenagers are sometimes drawn into the "battle ground" of marital disputes. The family stress at home makes concentrating on school a near impossibility. Moving from one area to another also causes havoc in young lives. Losing close friends, changing houses, schools, and communities can result in a child's dropping out of school.

5.   School Phobia: Although irrational fears strike only a very small percentage of the teenage population, they can be a factor in a student's decision to drop out. Some youngsters fear being mugged on campus, or feel humiliated by ridicule or worry about parent abandonment. These youngsters envision staying at home as a solution to their problem.

6.   Drugs: Teenagers who use dangerous drugs such as heroin, LSD, speed, barbiturates, and marijuana are at risk for dropping out. Help can come in the form of an alternative program that is not labeled "for drug users" but is part of the school's overall organization.

7.   Physical Illness: Youngsters who have suffered a physically disabling accident or illness frequently miss months of school while recuperating.

Unless an alternative form of education is offered, these youngsters are often forced to drop out of school, at least temporarily.

TEACHERS ARE AN IMPORTANT ELEMENT IN DROPOUT PREVENTION PROGRAMS

Students cannot be helped unless they are first diagnosed. Caring and alert teachers watch for youngsters who show symptoms of problems that may lead to their dropping out. Aside from friends, the teacher is frequently the person who spends the most time with a youngster. The following guidelines can help teachers spot youngsters who may need alternative education as a deterrent to dropping out of school.

Symptoms of Stress in At-Risk Students

1. Rapid weight loss (frequently associated with anorexia)
2. Excessive concern over exams or tests
3. Extreme anxiety over an occasion of tardiness or absence
4. Rapid weight gain in excess of twenty pounds
5. Departure from school when test results have just been reported, an awards assembly has just ended, or a lunch break has just begun or just ended
6. Asks excessive questions about homework assignments

Symptoms Found in Poor Role Model Students

1. A reputation for petty theft, vandalism, running with a gang, starting fights
2. Disrespectful language, including slang and swear words
3. Parents are unavailable, making it difficult for school personnel to talk with them
4. Poor grades
5. Consistently forgets to bring pencil, paper, or books to class
6. Frequent tardiness or truancy

Symptoms of Pregnancy

1. Weight loss followed a few months later by weight gain
2. Leaving class because of flu-like symptoms: nausea, vomiting, dizziness

3. Moodiness, including outbursts of tears during normal classroom activity

4. Inability to concentrate on classroom lessons

5. Frequent changes of friends

Symptoms of Family Disruption

1. Spends excessive amounts of time alone, ignoring classmates, and eating alone

2. Has a sad, sullen appearance and rarely laughs

3. Does not participate in after-school activities or field trips

4. Looks depressed and seems to daydream often

5. Is sometimes ridiculed by others

6. Has falling grades and increasing absences

7. Avoids discussing family matters

CASE HISTORY OF CONNIE: A REBELLIOUS TEENAGER

At sixteen, Connie was a truant and a runaway. She was rebellious and fought against the established rules and regulations of the school system. Her required appearance at a school attendance review board meeting only resulted in a referral to the juvenile authorities, as her rebellious nature would not allow her to respond to a demand that she return to traditional school. Hours spent in a girls' camp and on "Saturday clean-up" for truancy punishment did not work for Connie. Her "cure" needed to come in the form of counseling.

Connie walked into the counseling conference with a chip on her shoulder and a defiant look in her green eyes. She was twenty pounds overweight, wore too much makeup, and her bleached hair appeared dry and brittle. Physically, nature had not been kind to her. Suited up, she could have passed for a defensive lineman on the high school football squad. Her attitude and appearance pointed to her poor self-image.

It was easy to discern that the woman who walked behind Connie, as if attached by a tow rope, was her mother. They had the same physical characteristics and body formation.

It was immediately apparent that Connie was dead set against attending school of any kind. Her track record for attendance showed a pattern of constantly cutting classes, faking notes from her mother, smoking on campus, and generally disrupting the class when she did attend.

Confronting Connie with this evidence, we explained that the law required her to attend school and that we felt continuation school might fulfill her needs.

Required Peer Counseling at Continuation
School Begins the Healing Process

Typically, for the first few weeks after her referral Connie did come to school on a regular basis. Little was accomplished in the way of scholastic work, but the one-hour peer counseling sessions that she received offered valuable insights into her *pro tem* psyche. Connie felt that she should be in charge of her own life. She did not like rules and wanted to go and come as she pleased. Since she did not have rules and responsibilities at home, she felt she should not be required to respond to authority figures at school.

Six weeks after Connie began continuation school, she ran away from home. She started living with a girlfriend whose parents allowed the situation to continue without notifying Connie's mother. In an effort to locate Connie, the mother called the school and asked if she was in attendance. The next meeting between mother and child took place on the campus and resulted in a screaming match, including threatening gestures. As quickly as possible, Connie and her mother were ushered into the principal's office, where the possibility of professional counseling services was discussed. An appointment was made and the counselor was informed about Connie's statements during peer counseling.

The Beginning of Adult Awareness

Armed with a great deal of information about Connie, the counselor was able to get quickly to the essence of the problem. Although Connie had no respect for authority because of a lack of home training, unconsciously she really wanted rules and responsibility to make her feel loved and worthwhile. Actually, her poor self-image resulted from her parents' inability to parent her in a way that would encourage her to have good feelings about herself.

Connie grew to like attending continuation school because it made her feel as if she belonged to a family. Although she rebelled against traditional school regulations, the broad range of continuation rules allowed her enough leeway so that she could accustom herself to nearly complete acceptance of them. The small classes and individual attention were just the things Connie needed to promote her sense of self-worth. The short day allowed her to legally be absent in the afternoon when she needed to work at the job she had.

Once the counselor was able to pinpoint the reason for Connie's rebellion, the healing process commenced in Connie's own home.

Her life began to change. She took more of an interest in her personal appearance. She joined a physical fitness club, lost some weight, and made a greater effort at academic achievement. Discouraged at times, she would quit attending school temporarily, but always returned to the people whom she considered her "second family."

Shortly before Connie reached the age of twenty, she walked down the aisle of the school's auditorium and received her diploma.

Connie needed space, time to grow emotionally, and the freedom to form new relationships. Because of her emotionally weak state, she needed less academic pressure and more interaction with peers and adults. Continuation school offered these things to Connie. A selection of the right program for Connie and the caring personnel attached to this special school within the public school system saved Connie from becoming another high school dropout.

Work Experience Education   High School

STUDENT APPLICATION FOR WORK EXPERIENCE EDUCATION

PERSONAL INFORMATION

Student's Name _____ Birth Date _____ Grade: 11 12

Home Address _____ City _____ Zip _____ Phone _____

I would like W.E.E. included in my schedule of classes during periods 1 2 3 4 5 6
                                                                    (Circle periods)

I have previously earned credits for *IWE ____ *OWE ____ = Total Number of Credits _____

COURSE INFORMATION   *Verified by Counselor

	1st Semester	2nd Semester
Per.	Course	Course
1		
2		
3		
4		
5		
6		

* *
* Maximum of OWE/IWE credits is thirty (30) *
* including a maximum of twenty (20) OWE cr. *
* * * * * * * * ** * * * * * * * * * * *
I prefer to exchange the following courses for
Work Experience Education:

1._____

2._____

JOB INFORMATION (Please Print)

Employer _____   _____   _____
              Name of Business   Address   City   Zip   Phone

Person to contact: _____   Title: _____

Student's Job Title _____   Hourly Wage: _____

Time Schedule for each day of work: Example: Mon. __3–6 P.M.__

Mon. _____ Tues. _____ Wed. _____ Thurs. _____ Fri. _____ Sat. _____ Sun. _____

   Total hours per week _____ NOTE: Minors under eighteen (18) years of age shall not be permitted
   to work for more than four hours on any day when school is in session. Exception: Student enrolled
   in Work Experience Education may be permitted to work additional hours when approved by the
   W.E.E. Coordinator.

PARENTAL APPROVAL

We approve the school program including Work Experience Education and feel that the job

_____(student's name)_____ has will be beneficial to him/her.
I have read and understand the regulations for participation in Work Experience Education.

                    Parent's/Guardian's Signature: _____   __(date)__

- -

COUNSELOR RECOMMENDATION: COORDINATOR APPROVAL:

Recommended periods: _____ _____   Approved periods: _____ _____
Comments: _____   Comments: _____
_____   _____
_____   _____
Counselor's Signature   Date   Coordinator's Signature   Date

Form 3–1

OCCUPATIONAL WORK EXPERIENCE EDUCATION
PLAN OF TRAINING

Student _____ School _____

Occupational Goal _____

Employing Firm _____

Job Title _____

The following will be learned and experienced by the trainee on this job:

Knowledge _____

_____

_____

Skills _____

_____

_____

Tools, Machines, and Equipment _____

_____

_____

_____   _____
Signature of Employer or Supervisor   Date

_____   _____
Signature of Student   Date

_____   _____
Signature of Career/Work Experience   Date
    Education Coordinator

Form 3–2

STUDENT PARTICIPATION AGREEMENT

If my application for enrollment in Work Experience Education is approved, I agree to accept the following responsibilities in meeting the requirements for credits.

1. I have obtained a valid work permit and have it on file with my employer.

2. I will complete a training plan of learning objectives relevant to my job.

3. I will be enrolled in a minimum of three regular school courses (required of seniors) or four regular school courses (required of juniors) other than Work Experience.

4. I will be consistent in attendance on my job and in school.

5. I will carry out my duties in a responsible manner.

6. I will maintain my employment for the entire semester for which I am enrolled.

7. I will *inform* my Work Experience Education Coordinator immediately of *any changes or problems* in my job situation.

8. I will complete all assignments and attend scheduled group seminars.

    A. Group Seminars: Weekly

    B. Individual Learning Aid Packets (LAPS): As assigned

    C. Complete all related instruction assignments as required.

    D. Monthly work record due each month

9. I understand that if I fail to abide by any of the above the result may be a Drop F from the program.

10. I accept *all* of these conditions.

_____   _____   _____   _____
Student's Signature   Date   Parent's Signature   Date

Form 3–3

CONTINUATION REFERRAL FORM

Name of
Student _____   Home Phone _____

Address _____

Age _____ Birth Date _____ Grade _____

Mother's Name _____

Father's Name _____

Employer's Name _____ Work phone _____

Employer's Address _____

School Last Attended _____

Date of Referral to Continuation _____

Counselor _____ Referred by _____

Reasons student is being transferred to continuation school:

_____

_____

_____

_____

_____

Documents attached:

[ ] Attendance Records   [ ] Basic competency test results

Form 3–4

How Contract Independent Study Helps Retain High-Risk Students

Contract Independent Study is an alternative to classroom instruction that is consistent with the school district's curricula. It is not an alternative course of study, but it is separate from the traditional classroom programs. The course of study is based on a written contract, signed by the student, the parent or guardian, and the teacher. It is considered a full-time program, fulfilling full-time educational needs. Contract Independent Study is a good control measure for problem students who have been judged to be capable of learning at home by themselves, assisted by one or two hours per week of qualified teacher instruction and direction.

For the most part, independent study can be defined as "educational activity carried on by an individual seeking self-improvement, usually, but not always, self-initiated." Before proceeding with the initiation of an independent study program, however, an educator would be wise to examine carefully the causes behind any conflicts a student may be having at school.

WHO QUALIFIES FOR CONTRACT INDEPENDENT STUDY?

Many deviant teenagers lack the skill to study independently. Others thrive on it.

All students who undertake Contract Independent Study should have academic skills appropriate for the grade level for which they are attempting to earn credits. Secondary-level students with only primary-grade basic skills—in reading or math, for instance—should not be recommended to Contract Independent Study. By the same token, it has been demonstrated in practice that individuals with learning disabilities or handicaps usually are not successful either.

Most school districts establish an academic "plateau," or "floor," for eligibility. Many independent study programs give a standard reading test to help determine each applicant's qualifications.

When Does Contract Independent Study Help the Student?

The principal purpose of a Contract Independent Study program is to meet the educational needs of students who have experienced exceptional problems in adapting to the regular or traditional school system. The program is most often chosen for one of the following reasons:

1. As an alternative to expulsion

2. As a protective measure for a student who feels threatened by others while on campus

3. As a solution for hardship cases (for example, when an older sibling must provide care for younger members of the family)

4. As a way to provide continuity in case of forced or unavoidable absence from school

5. As a solution to truancy

6. As a "last chance" affiliation with the public school system

7. For athletes or performing arts students in professional training who find it difficult to keep to a regular classroom schedule

8. As a sustaining prop for a student who must work outside the home to help support a family

9. As a bridge from a drug rehabilitation program back to traditional school

A student may be referred to Contract Independent Study when it has been determined by the proper authorities to be in the student's best interest. It is a good idea to include a description of the student's educational needs along with the application, and for the referral to be made by a responsible member of the staff attached to the last school the student attended.

HOW THE INDEPENDENT STUDY PROGRAM FUNCTIONS

Children enrolled in the independent study program are usually assigned to a teacher who may also act as a counselor and who, in addition, assists the student to develop a personal plan of action based on individual needs and goals. There is no typical plan. The program is designed to provide a wide array of services, either directly or through referral to other agencies.

Some of the more common goals of independent study pupils are

1. To complete the necessary credits for a diploma
2. To study for and pass the state proficiency exam
3. To study for and pass the G.E.D. exam (see Chapter 11)
4. To stay in school until an age when school attendance will no longer be a legal requirement
5. To take a short respite from traditional schooling without losing credits
6. To be excusably absent (for example, traveling with the family), without losing credits

HOW TO IMPLEMENT THE INDEPENDENT STUDY PROGRAM

Step One

The local school board should adopt written policies and procedures for the program's operation. An advisory committee of teachers, parents, and administrators could draft this policy for presentation to the school board. (See Form 4–1 for guidelines.)

Step Two

Once the policy is approved, a person must be designated to choose the school site, provide overall direction for the program, and select staff.

A Contract Independent Study center can be located on campus in a classroom or in a portable building. It may also be located off campus, for instance in a commercial property.

The student-teacher ratio should be consistent with district policy (for example, one teacher per thirty students). A program with one hundred and fifty students may have two to four instructional aides, four full-time credentialed teachers, and a secretary.

Step Three

Record-keeping for attendance purposes must be in accordance with state attendance procedures and equal to traditional high school methods. Attendance credit is earned by the student and reported as a product of the ongoing instructional activities provided for by contract and supervised by teachers. The student actually substitutes equivalent educational time for regular classroom attendance through a contract with the supervising instructor.

Documentation of completed courses and attendance would include

1. A listing of regular work assignments (see Form 4–2)
2. A student work log showing hours spent on each activity (see Form 4–3)
3. A listing of completed assignments and academic credits earned and validated by the teacher's record and signature (see Forms 4–2 and 4–4)
4. The contract (see Form 4–5)
5. A signed agreement between student and school, stating the conditions of enrollment (see Form 4–6)
6. A permanent attendance record (use the local district's regulation form for this)
7. Locator and/or emergency information (use the local district's regulation form for this)

PROVISIONS AND COVENANTS OF THE CONTRACT

The contract is a written agreement that serves as the basic and initial document for audit functions and attendance accounting. The student's work is based on the contract which is written by the pupil and the teacher. This agreement governs such specifics as

1. The range of subjects a student will take
2. The frequency and length of meetings
3. The attempted course credit goals
4. The system of student work evaluation
5. The duration of each course
6. Major objectives to be reached by the student

SPECIFIC PURPOSES OF THE WEEKLY MEETING

Since Contract Independent Study is a substitute for regular classroom attendance, students are legally required to devote a specified amount of time per day to it. Most state laws mandate twenty hours a week for regular students and fifteen hours a week for continuation pupils (see Chapter 3 for more on continuation programs). All students are required to be enrolled in a minimum of four classes per semester and must meet with their instructor approximately once a week.

The purpose of the meeting is to

1. Verify that the student has studied for the required minimum length of time
2. Provide supervision and incentive
3. Provide instruction
4. Evaluate progress and grade completed work
5. Issue new work assignments
6. Resolve current problems

In order to control the number of study hours expended, students are asked to keep a log of the hours of work done at home and to submit this log to the instructor for perusal. The grading and assignment of work is based on the system used in the school from which the student originally came. (See Form 4–3.)

The requirements for graduation remain the same as for regular or traditional school.

ENROLLMENT PROCEDURES FOR CONTRACT INDEPENDENT STUDY

A principal, teacher, or administrator may refer a student to an independent study program when it is determined that it is in the student's best interest.

The determining factors are

1. The student's educational needs
2. The student's academic level of achievement
3. The student's academic level with respect to chronological age
4. The extent and circumstances of the problem that is expected to be alleviated by the change of environment
5. The cooperation and support of the parents or guardians

Once it is decided that a student should attend an independent study program, an orientation meeting should be arranged between the parent or guardian and the administrator.

The purpose of the meeting is to

1. Give a standard reading test to the student
2. Explain the conditions of the program

3. Get all the paperwork signed by the parent or guardian. This includes the contract, locator form, and anything else used in registration

4. Issue work assignments and textbooks

5. Set up a meeting time and place

6. Evaluate the transcript of the student and set up educational goals

THE REFERRAL COMMITTEE: AN IMPORTANT FEATURE OF THE PROGRAM

One of the most important aspects of the independent study program is its referral service. The staff stays in touch with such special area programs as reading clinics, employment agencies, apprenticeship opportunities, and rehabilitation services, so that students in need can quickly find help.

In some cases, students who have been undergoing rehabilitation or who have been in a private school may wish to use independent study for support during their transition to traditional school.

Referrals by high school counselors provide the majority of the candidates for independent study. Teachers who observe unusual classroom behavior provide counselors with names of youngsters who may need help. The counselors, in turn, interview the youngsters and seek an avenue of educational assistance for the more troubled among them. (See Form 4–7.)

All observant teachers have the ability to spot troubled youths when familiar with the known signs of impending vexations. However, drug dependency is one of the more difficult problems to identify. The following list of warning signs can be helpful:

1. Abrupt changes in behavior, such as loss of interest in sports or other activities

2. Increased truancy with lack of parent awareness; student may fake notes from parents

3. Moodiness

4. Disinterest in the opposite sex

5. Carelessness in appearance, which may or may not include an appearance of intoxication

6. A tendency to appear lazy (student may sit and look off into space)

7. Loss of appetite and, usually, a quick loss of weight

8. Unkind remarks about friends who were once their "buddies"; acquisition of new friends

9. Evasive answers to teacher's questions about tardiness

10. Refusal to make whereabouts known to parent or school authorities after being absent

11. Isolation behind a locked door for extended periods of time

12. Mysterious disappearance of valuable items in the classroom that may be worth easy money at a pawn shop

13. Inability to control emotions; uncontrollable laughter or crying for no apparent reason

14. Unusual marks on arms, such as small scars or black and blue discolorations that are explained with vague answers

The following case history will demonstrate how the independent study program was instrumental in the turnaround, rehabilitation, and dropout retrieval of a minor drug addict who had managed to manipulate the school system for many years.

CASE HISTORY OF LINDA: A DRUG ADDICT

Linda was referred to the independent study program by the high school counseling office.

During our initial talk, she was responsive and nonaggressive. She seemed more than willing to give the program a try. I signed her up for the basic classes and terminated the interview on a congenial note. Seven days later she was back with her assignment completed.

I was delighted.

In the ensuing weeks, a close rapport was established between us. She progressed so well, precedent dictated that I recommend her as capable of going back to traditional school.

Her panic was instantly obvious when I informed her of my intent.

I knew then that there was more behind her behavior pattern than a simple dislike of traditional school routine. I managed to coax out her story.

Background Information Is an Important Diagnostic Tool

Linda had been introduced to marijuana by her older brother and had been on drugs since the age of ten. She used them all, starting with marijuana. Later she escalated to the habitual use of barbiturates (commonly known by the slang terms "reds," "pink ladies," "bennies," "pep pills," "yellow jackets," and "speed").

By the time Linda got to high school, her reputation had preceded her. All the kids on campus knew who and what she was. Linda, who had been looking forward to a new start in a different school, became so despondent over this situation that she played hooky frequently in the months following. She would go to a nearby public park just to sit and think, and indulge in her habit.

The Unheeded, Silent Cry for Help

As early as the age of eleven, and throughout her junior high school years, Linda engaged in promiscuous sex, suffered beatings by drug-crazed partners, and went through the humiliations and degradations of being caught shoplifting. She did this to support a drug habit that her regular allowance was unable to cover.

Linda's mother and father were concerned about her behavior, but she successfully parried their questions and inquiries with made-up stories. Too grown up to blatantly ask for help, yet too young and inexperienced to cope on her own, she continued to struggle to solve her own problems, all the while secretly hoping that someone would recognize her plight. Her parents were not wise enough to realize that their daughter was silently crying for assistance.

Linda knew that what she was doing was wrong, and she wanted out. But ensconced as she was within her particular peer group, and hovered over by other drug addicts, she felt she had little or no chance of breaking free as long as she was forced to go to traditional school. In a last, desperate attempt to rid herself of the bad influence of her environment, she had quit attending school altogether.

Since Linda's violations of society's regulations appeared in her file simply as a breach of school attendance requirements, she was considered a truant, nothing more.

Four Ways the Independent Study Program Helped Linda

The independent study program took Linda away from the influence of her drug-addicted peer group and gave her a chance to build her own internal rehabilitation forces.

It exposed her to a concerned and trained educator who recognized the symptoms of a long-hidden problem that was gradually eroding her life—a person who "heard" Linda's silent cry for help and who was not satisfied with half-truths or content to accept flimsy excuses.

It furnished her with a sanctioned opportunity to study at home, in a less hazardous environment, where she could successfully pursue her desire to better herself.

It turned Linda around, starting her on the road to recovery and set an example for others in her group, as well as all groups, who might need help, or who might be on the verge of following Linda's former path.

Linda remained in the independent study program. She studied for—and passed—the state proficiency test, then continued to gain credits toward graduation. When she reached the age of nineteen, her dogged determination finally earned her that high school diploma.

BOARD POLICY
GUIDELINES FOR IMPLEMENTING INDEPENDENT STUDY

These guides are in accordance with State Administrative Code

I. *Definition, Rationale, and Scope*

A. *Definition:* Independent Study is an alternative to classroom instruction consistent with the district's course of study.

B. *Rationale:* There are times when it is in a student's best interest to include in his or her program Independent Study, in addition to, or instead of, regular course assignments. The board has recognized the need to provide opportunities for Independent Study as part of the district's instructional program as set forth in their policy statement of ___(date)___ .

C. *Scope:* An individual student or group of students, may engage in Independent Study on or off campus. An Independent Study program may range from an activity conducted as part of a regular class to an activity completely separate from the regular program.

D. An Independent Study program or project need not be limited in time or geographical distance from school site.

II. *Procedures for Implementation of Independent Study*

A. *Supervision:* (1) Each school shall designate a certified person to be coordinator of Independent Study. The coordinator shall be responsible for the administration and supervision of the Independent Study Program. (2) Independent Study programs must be under the primary but general supervision of a school-certificated staff member; however, immediate supervision of an activity can be undertaken by other individuals who have volunteered, but who are not directly affiliated with the school district, such as parents, students, or other community members.

B. *Coordination:* Each school or program shall develop guidelines for necessary procedures, including, but not limited to:
1. Identifying students appropriate for the program.
2. Enrolling students in the program.
3. Monitoring students' progress.
4. Evaluating students' learning.

C. *Written Agreements:* (1) Independent Study shall be based on a written agreement signed by the student, the student's parents or legal guardian for minor students, and the certificated supervisor, and any other person who has direct responsibility to provide instructional assistance to the student. (2) This agreement shall include, but not be limited to:
1. The title and statement of the major objectives of the course of study to be undertaken.
2. The kinds of activities intended to reach the objectives.
3. The method by which progress toward the objectives will be evaluated.
4. The duration of the Independent Study contract.
5. The manner, frequency, time, and place of reporting progress.

D. *Records:* Records shall be maintained on each school site and shall include, but not be limited to:
   1. A copy of this board policy statement in current condition and pertinent administrative regulations.
   2. A file of all agreements, fulfilled and unfulfilled.
   3. A list of students who have participated in Independent Study, showing the credit/units attempted by and awarded to each student per agreement.
   4. The number of students who successfully fulfill a contract or agreement.
   5. Grade and/or evaluation of units of study comparable to classroom work.
   6. Samples of student work that demonstrate quality and scope of study, especially for atypical student programs.

Note: Additional examples of board policy for Independent Study may be obtained by contacting districts with existing independent study programs.

Form 4–1

WEEKLY ASSIGNMENT SHEET

Teacher: _____

Student: _____

Day: _____

Date: _____

Time: _____

Course Titles	DATE:	ASSIGNMENT	HRS.	ASSIGNMENT COMPLETED	HRS.	COMMENTS

Teacher's initails:_____ Total Hours Assigned:_____ Total Hours Completed:_____ Attendance Period:

Date work Completed _____ Total Days Granted:_____ _____

Form 4–2

STUDENT LOG

NAME _____   TEACHER _____

Beginning Date _____   COURSE TITLE _____

Ending Date _____   Total Time _____

In order to receive a grade for this course, you must enter all time spent on the course, both at The Center and at home. Enter each test you take and the grade on the test. When logging in time spent, please indicate A.M. or P.M.

Book Title, Tape, Filmstrip, Text—be sure to indicate Chapters & Pages	Date	From	To	Hours	Min.

TOTAL HOURS _____

I certify that the log represents an accurate amount of the time spent on the stated assignments.

_____   _____
PARENT'S SIGNATURE   STUDENT'S SIGNATURE

Form 4–3

CLASS/SUBJECT ASSIGNMENT RECORD

Name _____ Date Initiated _____ through

Course Title _____ Credits Attempted _____

Teacher _____ Check-in day _____

Title(s) of Text(s)/Book(s) to be used: _____

Specific skill(s) that student is to work on (where applicable) _____

_____

Date	Chapters worked on this week:	Hours this week:
1- __/__/__	_____	_____
2- __/__/__	_____	_____
3- __/__/__	_____	_____
4- __/__/__	_____	_____
5- __/__/__	_____	_____
6- __/__/__	_____	_____
7- __/__/__	_____	_____
8- __/__/__	_____	_____
9- __/__/__	_____	_____
10- __/__/__	_____	_____
11- __/__/__	_____	_____
12- __/__/__	_____	_____
13- __/__/__	_____	_____
14- __/__/__	_____	_____
15- __/__/__	_____	_____
16- __/__/__	_____	_____
17- __/__/__	_____	_____
18- __/__/__	_____	_____

_____ _____ _____ _____
Student's Signature   Supervisor's Signature   Credits Earned   Grade

_____
Completion Date

Form 4—4

CONTRACT FOR INDEPENDENT STUDY

NAME _____ GRADE _____

ADDRESS _____ AGE _____ BIRTHDATE _____

CITY _____ ZIP _____ PHONE _____

INDEPENDENT STUDY CONTRACT CATEGORY (in addition to HIGH SCHOOL DIPLOMA)

( ) On-Campus Study   ( ) ROP/OWE/IWE   ( ) Community Lab   Entry Date _____

( ) Off-Campus Study   ( ) GED/CHSPE   ( ) Night School   Leave Date _____

( ) Educational Travel   ( ) Other _____

OBJECTIVES:

The following subject areas will be attempted during the 1985-86 school year. All course objectives will be consistent with the guidelines established in the district course curriculum guide. Fifteen (15) hours of work equals one (1) unit of credit. Student contracts and weekly agreement forms contain additional descriptions of student's goals & objectives.

SUBJECT	CREDITS TO BE ATTEMPTED	SUBJECT	CREDITS TO BE ATTEMPTED
_____	_____	_____	_____
_____	_____	_____	_____
_____	_____	_____	_____

SCHEDULED TEACHER/STUDENT MEETING

Student and Teacher agree to meet according to the following schedule:

Time _____ Day _____

Location: _____ (School Name) _____

EVALUATION ACTIVITIES

. Assignment Completed

. Demonstration/Skills

. Written Test/Report

. Student Log

. Oral/Written Presentation

. Other _____

_____

AGREEMENT: We have read the terms of this contract and hereby agree to all the conditions set forth within.

SIGNATURES /

STUDENT __/__/__   TEACHER __/__/__   PARENT/GUARDIAN __/__/__

PROGRAM ADMINISTRATOR __/__/__   IMMEDIATE SUPERVISOR __/__/__

CERTIFICATION:

	Fall Semester					Spring Semester			
DATE	SUBJECT	GRADE	INIT.	CREDITS EARNED	DATE	SUBJECT	GRADE	INIT.	CREDITS EARNED
___	___	___	___	___	___	___	___	___	___
___	___	___	___	___	___	___	___	___	___
___	___	___	___	___	___	___	___	___	___
___	___	___	___	___	___	___	___	___	___
___	___	___	___	___	___	___	___	___	___
___	___	___	___	___	___	___	___	___	___

TOTAL CREDITS EARNED:_____   DATE RECORDED_____   TEACHER'S SIG._____

Form 4–5

NAME _____

CONDITIONS OF ENROLLMENT

I. *Scheduled Meetings:* Student agrees to meet with assigned staff member at least once a week for one to two hours. It is the responsibility of the student to reschedule appointments. *Failure to report to two (2) consecutive appointments may result in termination of this agreement.*

II. *Minimum Study Requirements:* Student agrees to complete a minimum of twenty (20) hours per week of homework. Credit can be issued only after a student meets with a teacher/supervisor. (NOTE: Hourly requirements may be varied by individual contract within state guidelines.)

AGREEMENT

I. *Student:* I have read the terms and conditions of this Enrollment Agreement and hereby agree to *all* conditions and limitations set forth. I understand that failure to report to my regularly scheduled appointments with the agreed-upon program may result in a referral to the school attendance review board and/or other agencies and revoking the intradistrict transfer back to my home school.

If I am placed on the inactive list, I understand that my work permit will be revoked until such time as I reenroll and do satisfactory work.

I understand any violation of the student conduct and discipline policy of the unified school district or failure to meet contract requirements is cause for dismissal from the program.

I understand that I must participate in one or more of the following: community service, employment, or directed project.

_____
Student's Signature   Date

II. *Parent:* I understand that the major objective of independent study is to provide an off-campus education for my son/daughter. I also understand:
    a. That individual course objectives are evaluated in the same manner that they would be if my son/daughter were enrolled in a regular school program.
    b. That unless otherwise indicated above, a teacher or supervisor will meet with my son/daughter on a weekly basis to direct and measure progress in the program, with the time and location of meeting to be determined by the teacher or supervisor and the student.

I have read the terms and conditions of this Enrollment Agreement and hereby agree to *all* conditions and limitations set forth.

_____
Parent's Signature   Date

III. *Enrollment Approval:*

_____   _____
Teacher   Date   Supervisor   Date

REFERRAL FORM

School/Program/Agency	Date of Referral

BACKGROUND INFORMATION

Student	Birth Date	Ethnicity	Sex	Age

HO #   Parent/Guardian

Address   Phone (H)   (W)

Grade   Counselor

Language Spoken by Student   Primary Home Language

REASON(S) FOR REFERRAL:

_____

_____

PREVIOUS ACTION(S) TAKEN:

_____

_____

EDUCATIONAL NEEDS OF THE STUDENT

Credits to Date	Subject	Need	Credits to Date	Subject	Need
	English			Physical Ed.	
	Science			Electives	
	Soc. Studies			CHS. P.E. Prep.	
	Mathematics			GED Prep.	

ADDITIONAL INFORMATION

Group Test Data: _____

Test: _____ Date taken: _____

Results:

Mathematics	%
RDG/LANG/ENG	%
Social Studies	%
Science	%

CONSENT TO REFERRAL:

_____ Principal/Asst. Principal
Signature

_____ Counselor
Signature

_____ Other:

FOR OFFICE USE ONLY

☐ Accepted   ☐ Not Accepted

☐ Other Action:

_____

Form 4-7

============================ **Chapter 5** ============================

How Vocational Training Methods Help Needy Students Finish High School

Most educators are familiar with high school home economics and shop classes in which young people are taught to sew, cook, and even to maintain and repair autos. This type of curriculum was especially designed to give students the background needed for the daily experiences of life. They are taught in almost every high school in the United States and are generally referred to as job-skill classes. However, it is wise to keep in mind that they remain essentially basic, and while they are instrumental in forming good foundations, they seldom provide the skills required for a high-paying position.

To increase the availability of these basic job-skill classes, many school districts have a separate facility where students can acquire the skills they need for jobs such as secretary, girl or man Friday, auto mechanic, nurse's aide, or food service worker. This is in lieu of more advanced academic studies for which the student may not have an interest or aptitude.

In providing this type of education, it is not the intention of the public school to compete with the commercial trade schools, but to present goal-oriented students with an alternative to the usual college-preparatory curriculum.

It must be recognized that for a number of high school students there is no substitute for the training received at a good trade school. Educators and programmers are to be congratulated for the successes they have achieved among young people in this field and for literally preventing dropout in many cases.

HOW THE VOCATIONAL TRAINING PROGRAM FUNCTIONS

A student in a vocational training program attends classes for two hours a day. Under the best conditions, and for control purposes, this is generally in a building or structure that is separate from, but on or near the regular high school campus. However, classes have been successfully conducted in more remote facilities and the inability to locate the classes on or near the regular campus should not be allowed to deter the program. The remaining two to four hours of the school day are spent on the regular curriculum, including English, math, and science, in classrooms on a regular high school campus.

While attending vocational training classes, the student actually performs job duties, working beside a qualified journeyman, emulating, assisting, and learning. Up-to-date vocational centers have simulated work stations. For best results, these are small, task-oriented areas that are equipped with the necessary tools and instructional materials. Training is offered (often via books and cassettes) in the skills required for occupations such as machinist, plumber, and auto mechanic; for students with more mathematical or creative aptitude, there are classes in accounting, advertising, and communications to prepare students for these careers. The variety and quality of what is offered are limited only by the program's budget.

For a great number of students, these classes offer a once-in-a-lifetime experience, as well as a once-in-a-lifetime opportunity.

WHICH STUDENTS QUALIFY FOR VOCATIONAL EDUCATION?

Youths fourteen through eighteen years of age who may be on the verge of dropping out are the largest source of candidates. These students, who are generally found to be truants and troublemakers, and who are academically behind their chronological age achievement potential, often find in vocational classes an outlet for their pent-up energies and emotions, together with a range of goal-achievement possibilities commensurate with their own self-image. Vocational training provides these students with a feeling of accomplishment when they see the tangible results of their labor—and they stay in school.

Another potential candidate is the so-called "regular" student who is more or less a docile conformist, but who is simply overwhelmed by the stringent curriculum requirements of traditional school. Young people in this category constitute a much smaller candidate pool, however, since some of them ultimately adjust and continue to follow traditional channels. The few who are selected for the vocational educational program as a remedial alternative to prevent dropout generally find new enthusiasm and achieve success.

A third category consists of the children of migrant workers. Because these children are constantly on the move and unable to attend school regularly, they receive a poor basic education and become discouraged. Many can ultimately go on to productive careers by taking advantage of the vocational educational program instead of dropping out.

THE VOCATIONAL TRAINING PROGRAM AS A DROPOUT PREVENTION MEDIUM

The principal purpose of vocational training is to provide an opportunity for youngsters to develop job skills that will allow them to make a smooth transition from school to the workplace. Many teenagers, feeling the loss of pride and self-respect that comes with failure in school, view money as the solution to their problems. The vision of owning an automobile, wearing designer clothes, and gaining peer status is foremost in their minds. The desire for accomplishment and recognition is so acute that some lose sight of the fact that honest money can be acquired only through productive effort, and that in order to perform well-paid labor, the worker must have the skills to match. Many drop out of school when making money becomes more important, necessary or attractive than sitting in a classroom. However, this simply compounds their dilemma. Once out of school, they have little or no chance to learn the skills necessary to qualify them for employment that will pay the money they so earnestly desire.

Vocational training is attractive to these youngsters because it allows them to make visible progress toward their ultimate aim while remaining in school. At the same time, it exposes them to a variety of "hands-on" work opportunities and provides the specialized knowledge they will need to earn money later. Being able to actually see and touch, the results of their labor is often an incentive to potential dropouts to suffer through the academic portions of the curriculum. They visualize the two hours of vocational instruction as leading to well-paid work that they enjoy.

There are several other benefits the potential dropout may reap from the vocational training program. Among these are

1. Pride of achievement
2. Self-understanding
3. Decision-making skills

4. Responsible work behavior and attitudes
5. The confidence to think independently
6. Credits toward a high school diploma (in an amount determined by the local administration)

HOW TO IMPLEMENT A VOCATIONAL EDUCATIONAL PROGRAM

Generally, the governing board of a school district must set the scope of the vocational educational program and define the student body it will include. To set the process in motion:

1. Scout out a school or classroom site.
2. Identify potential candidates among students.
3. Present an introduction proposal to the school board.
4. After the introductory proposal is approved, develop and submit a budget proposal based on need and projected ADA (average daily attendance). To estimate the ADA appropriation, check the amount appropriated per ADA in the high school and multiply it by the projected number of vocational training students for the coming fiscal year.
5. Investigate possible funding sources:
    a. Find flexible ways to utilize existing laws and programs and to create cooperation between agencies and new programs.
    b. Check to see if your current state statutes authorize funds for apprenticeship programs. Many do.
    c. Suggest bidding for apportionments at the end of the year.
    d. Look into the possibility that your state rewards districts who expand "opportunity" classrooms and offer extensive alternative choices.
    e. Contact your federal and state legislators for help.

See the sample proposal in Form 5–1.

STAFFING THE CENTER

The teachers who are asked to work at the vocational education center should have a sincere concern for the kinds of students who need this special help. Although some of the students in the program will not be at risk for dropping out, a high percentage of those enrolled can be expected to be potential dropouts. A ratio of one credentialed teacher to every thirty or thirty-five students is the general rule. This ratio, however, depends on established district guidelines. The ratio of uncredentialed instructors must be kept flexible and will usually fluctuate according to need.

Volunteers are an important element. It has proven to be a good idea to recruit persons from the immediate community who have the vocational skills most in demand. These volunteers supply a large portion of the manually skilled personnel who demonstrate techniques and methods for the students. The accredited, full-time teachers are not expected, nor should they try, to lead the students in every job-training exercise. It has been demonstrated that this practice usually ends in failure for the program.

RECORD-KEEPING

Record-keeping for attendance purposes should be in line with, and equal to, methods used in any other classroom in the district. There is no reason to deviate from the district method of attendance accounting. Attendance credit is earned for each day the student is in class for the minimum number of hours per day as prescribed by the state. The vocational education center should be accorded the same status as a traditional classroom.

INNOVATIVE WAYS TO GET HARD-TO-FIND HOUSING FOR AN UNDERFUNDED VOCATIONAL EDUCATIONAL JOB CENTER

When instituting a vocational educational program, many educators become discouraged by the lack of funding for the new quarters they feel are necessary for the project. In reality, this is a minor problem. While funding is always lacking for new construction, *recurring* expenses are generally budgeted or funded from stabilized sources, especially if they are viewed as reasonable and not excessive. The following are some things you can try if conventional funding methods hit a snag and you really want to get that much-needed vocational educational program functioning:

1. Practically all communities have vacant buildings with owners who are in search of good tenants. An old fire station, courthouse, or outgrown city hall may very well provide the appropriate site for the project.

2. Look for an obsolete, even abandoned, residence in a developing industrial area of town, or for a commercial property that has remained empty for a long time.

3. Search for portable buildings that can be easily moved.

4. Keep in mind that funds will be more readily available if the cost is kept to a minimum. Remodeling a building is usually much less expensive than erecting a new building. Buildings can generally be

used during the remodeling process. Try to avoid excessive costs of new construction that might tend to render the program financially unfeasible.

ENROLLMENT PROCEDURES FOR THE VOCATIONAL EDUCATIONAL CENTER

Once established in the district, vocational education should be made available to *all* students in grades nine through twelve. All teachers, counselors, and administrators within the district should be endowed with the authority to refer students for admission to the program, providing it has been determined by the referring party that such a move is in the best interest of the student. (Refer to Form 5–2.)

Determining factors for referral usually include, but are not limited to, the following:

1. The student's educational needs. This includes such things as an evaluation of the student's reading scores, amount of credit earned to date, classes needed for graduation, goals after graduation

2. The student's school history, including attendance, behavior, and level of academic achievement

3. The extent and circumstances of any past or current problems, either directly or indirectly related to school

4. The student's own reasons for desiring to become a part of the program

Once it has been definitely determined that a particular student will be included in the vocational education program, the high school counselor should be notified and should

1. Make the appropriate adjustments in the youngster's daily schedules

2. Prepare the agreement form (see Form 5–3) for execution

3. Give the student a time and date for starting the program

What About Community Referrals?

It is most important that the school attendance review committee, together with all district high schools, community centers, and other civic and district programs, be notified that a vocational education program has been established and that a Job Center is available. If the program is to be fully utilized as a dropout prevention tool, high-risk students who meet the enrollment criteria must be counseled accordingly and referred to the program.

Counselors in all district schools should be supplied with complete information on enrollment procedures and criteria so that they can properly advise students.

A good way to do this is to advertise by posting Form 5–2 on the bulletin board in every school within the district, by passing it out to students, and by asking those who receive it as a handout to pass it along to other interested parties.

THE IMPORTANCE OF VOCATIONAL EDUCATION AS AN INTEGRAL PART OF HIGH SCHOOL LEARNING

With the trend from rural to city living, vocational skills are less likely to be taught at home, simply because children no longer work for the family. In rural areas, young people are needed to harvest the crop, run the family store, manage the books, or tend the livestock. The skills learned during the performance of these chores are useful for a lifetime.

Today, vocational skills are sometimes taught in the home, but the practice is not as prevalent as it once was. For example, when your automobile breaks down, you have two choices: fix it yourself, or take it to a professional auto mechanic.

The parents who choose to repair the auto themselves will be doing their youngsters a favor if they invite them to watch or participate. In this manner, the skill of the parent is passed on to younger members of the family who, in turn, may eventually pass it on to their own children. However, if the parent does not know how to repair the automobile and a professional mechanic must be retained, the opportunity for the child to learn this manual skill is eliminated. Unfortunately, this is happening more and more, simply because city living makes it easy to rely on the skills of people outside the family for help. Consequently, fewer and fewer children learn manual skills.

The accelerating importance of craft and trade skills can be discerned from a glance at the newspaper want ads. These reveal only a modest number of job opportunities for technically skilled professionals such as teachers, bankers, engineers, analysts, and other liberal arts majors. At the same time, there seems to be an overabundance of jobs for electricians, machinists, computer programmers, mechanics, dental assistants, and many of the other skilled trades.

It makes good sense, then, to gear the vocational classes that are offered in the local high school to the demands of the community in which the school is situated, and to have these courses focus on the needs of local industry. Since the work-experience portion of the vocational education program will most likely be gained from local sources, attention to their needs will give graduating students their best chance for future employment. Past experience has shown that a combination of traditional academic skills and vocational skills gives youngsters a much higher success rate for finding and keeping good, well-paying jobs. With this kind of educational background to rely on, students entering the work force have a head start.

CASE HISTORY OF SHARON: A TRUANT

Sharon was a typical all-American girl with a B-grade academic average. For three years she was a star athlete who played center on the basketball team and at the same time held a class office. She had peer status and was well thought of by the entire school staff.

In her senior year, Sharon became a truancy statistic.

This behavior was so unusual for Sharon that a home visit was immediately scheduled. A few well-directed inquiries disclosed that Sharon had been exposed to some family problems that had put her on the verge of physical illness and emotional exhaustion, making her incapable of keeping up with her senior studies.

The story came from her mother.

The Cause and Effect of Sharon's Lifestyle Disruption

Sharon's father and mother were high school sweethearts. Her mother had left school early in order to marry. For twenty years her father had been a good parent and husband and had supported the family well with his job as a truck driver. Then, without warning, he had walked out on the whole family. The parents were divorcing.

The mother, with no job skills, no high school diploma, and no money to start over, could not find a job. She was left with no way to support the family and was fearful of losing the home. She was finally forced to take the only type of job she could qualify for and went to work in a fast food restaurant. Sharon, too, had taken a job in the same restaurant. Sharon's shift was from 3:00 P.M. till midnight, which made it very difficult for her to rise early enough in the morning to attend classes on time. She often overslept and felt exhausted when she was awake. Frequently she stayed at home instead of going to school, in order to be able to continue her job, knowing how badly the family needed the money.

Sharon became depressed. As time went on and no solution presented itself, her depression deepened. She lost interest in the highlight of her life, which was basketball, and worst of all, she lost her desire to graduate.

The School Counselor's Evaluation and Recommendations

Because of Sharon's previously good study habits and attendance record, she needed only a few more class credits to earn her diploma and graduate. With the exception of a senior government class, all her required studies were complete. During a discussion of options with Sharon and her mother, it was determined that it would be in Sharon's best interest to enroll in the vocational training program for two hours each afternoon, in addition to attending the important government class she still needed. This was accomplished by rescheduling Sharon's daily activity routine so that she could sleep in the morning, attend her vocational food services class in the early afternoon, complete her government class, and still be on time for her job. This reoriented her life and put her in control, making it possible for her to hold down a full-time job while finishing her education.

As an added reward, Sharon was also learning important management skills in her vocational food services classes—skills, she realized, that would someday enable her to operate her own fast food restaurant and insure her employment in the future, despite the fact that operating such a chain might not be her lifetime achievement goal.

Vocational Training as a Gateway to a Productive Future

Sharon did not become a high school dropout. She graduated and went on to play basketball at a local junior college. If the alternative public school program had not been available to her, Sharon's story might have ended differently. Considering her age, the SARB committee in all likelihood would have acted slowly, or perhaps not at all. Even a letter from the SARB reiterating the requirements of the state law would likely have been ignored by the parents because of the turmoil within the family.

At this point, Sharon is grateful for the skills she learned in the vocational classes she attended. They have literally given her a new outlook, as well as a new lifestyle. She advanced to, and became involved with, a new and different group of peers, fresh surroundings, and an engrossing occupation that allowed her to momentarily escape from her troubles at home. Whether or not she goes on to higher education, her future has been stabilized, and she is a productive asset to society.

CASE HISTORY OF MARY: DAUGHTER OF A MIGRANT WORKER

The youngest of six siblings, Mary was eighteen years old at the end of her senior year. She needed to make up one more semester to earn a diploma. She had missed one semester in her junior year when she dropped out temporarily to have a baby and failed to take advantage of the pregnant minors program. (See Chapter 9.)

Mary's parents had worked in the fields most of their lives and had never found the time to obtain more than a third-grade education. Her sisters and brothers followed in the footsteps of their parents, all leaving school at the age of sixteen with the equivalent of a fourth-grade education. Formal education, beyond simple reading and writing, held a low position on their priority list and was considered an unnecessary waste of leisure time.

Despite her family's common attitude regarding higher education, there were three factors that kept Mary going to school:

1. An extreme dislike for the type of work her parents performed and expected her to perform

2. Constant encouragement from school counselors to continue

3. Peers whose company she thoroughly enjoyed

Mary's gentle nature made her well-loved by her fellow students and teachers. She possessed the gift of articulateness and had a natural charisma that inspired those who knew her with the hope that she would strive to become successful.

Then Mary became a dropout.

Why Mary Left School

Working as a farm laborer for thirty years had taken its toll on Mary's mother, Rose. Rose's health had suddenly failed and surgery was necessary to preserve her life. Complete bed rest was essential during recovery, and with Rose bedridden, the family income was suddenly halved. Unexpected medical bills added to the financial burden. Mary felt that the solution to the problem rested on her shoulders. She was determined to earn money by going to work.

Taking on the time-consuming responsibility of finding a job conflicted with Mary's continuing attendance at school. Her interest diminished further when she realized that her peers, who were one of the chief stabilizing factors in her educational success so far, were soon going to graduate and would be entering the job market or going on to college, leaving her behind. It was suddenly brought home to her what her temporary one-semester dropout had cost her. She became depressed, fearing she was slipping into the same rut of hard labor she had seen her own parents endure. She saw her own future in the image of her mother, uneducated, near poverty, and in poor health. As her depression deepened, she shunned society and retreated within her own home. At the start of the fall semester, she failed to show up for classes.

Remedial Actions Undertaken to Bring About Mary's Recovery

When a home call was made, Mary opened up and disclosed her troubles to the counselor. The reaction was immediate. There was no doubt that the school could help. In a speedily arranged diagnostic consultation session, it was concluded that the following things would be best for Mary:

1. Vocational training that would enable her to get a job other than farm labor

2. More free time at home in which to care for her baby and her mother

3. Employment in a good-paying job so she could help with family finances

Mary was persuaded to visit the counselor's office so that the options open to her could be explained and a vocational guide test administered.

When the results of the test demonstrated an aptitude for nurturing, she was steered toward a medical records training program. She commenced attending classes two hours each day, and grasped the material so well that her eventual success seemed assured from the start. Nursing appeared to be Mary's forte. Within a month, she was hired by the local hospital and began using her acquired skills for four hours each day as a paid employee.

Mary's paying job allowed her to receive work-experience credits as well as credit for vocational education classes, and she was delighted to be earning units toward her high school diploma once again.

With only seven hours of her day occupied with school and gainful employment, Mary found the free time she needed for home duties. In the morning, before the bus came, she was able to help her mother with breakfast, prepare her own child for the day, and attend to her mother. After vocational classes, there was time for lunch at home. By utilizing the city transportation system for her journey to and from the hospital, she was home in time to help her mother with the evening chores and to tuck her own son in his bed at night.

How Vocational Training Can Lead to a Brighter Life

At last report, Mary's hospital job had become full time, and she was still accumulating credits toward her diploma. Although she had not yet been able to complete all of the classes required for her diploma, she planned to make use of the adult education program. (See Chapter 11 for more on adult education.)

BOARD POLICY

INITIAL PROPOSAL FOR VOCATIONAL TRAINING CENTER

I. Project Title—Definition
   A. A vocational education center creates an alternative to the academic classroom. It allows the student to spend two periods a day at simulated work stations that provide job training.
   B. An individual student, or group of students, will have the opportunity to attend the center during *regular* school hours.

II. Project Projection
   A. There are times when it is in the student's best interest to enroll in an alternative to academic study. Students who are on the verge of dropping out may be induced to stay by the offer of on-the-job training as part of their regular school day.
   B. The vocational education center will function as a viable dropout prevention program, which should result in a more stabilized attendance record and therefore in increased revenues for the district.

III. Procedures
   A. Each school district must develop and adhere to guideline procedures for:
      1. Identifying students who are candidates for the program.
      2. Enrolling students in the program.
      3. Monitoring students enrolled in the program.
      4. Evaluating student learning and achievement.
   B. Record-keeping can follow regular classroom attendance monitoring procedures.

IV. Rationale
   Vocational training centers offer instruction in a broad range of occupations. The program requires both manual dexterity and academic achievement. Several things will become apparent to students participating in this program:
      1. They will more easily comprehend the vital relationship between *academic work* and *employment,* which will reinforce their motivation to continue in school.
      2. They will see how routine schoolwork relates to future, long-range employment.
      3. They will be more content when manually employed.

Note: As optional items, the proposal may also include: (1) procedures for implementation, and (2) a detailed plan for evaluating success.

Form 5–1

UNION HIGH SCHOOL DISTRICT

NAME OF PROGRAM ___VOCATIONAL TRAINING CENTER___

TELEPHONE NUMBER _____

POPULATION SERVED ___District students in grades 9–12___

HOURS OF OPERATION ___8:00 A.M. to 3:00 P.M.___

PURPOSE OF PROGRAM ___1. Instruction in work-related English and math.___

2. Career education through class work and job samples

3. Provision of alternative school location and atmosphere

4. Opportunity for obtaining on-the-job experience through volunteer and paid

   work.

CREDIT OFFERED ___Same as comprehensive school___

PREREQUISITE (IF ANY) ___None___

METHOD OF ENTRY ___Counselor referral/interview with parent & student___

LENGTH OF PROGRAM One semester. With counselor and program permission,

student may return for second semester.

WHOM TO CONTACT

_____

_____

SPECIAL FEATURES ___"Hands-on" classroom experience of more than thirty occu-___
pations gives students a chance to explore different fields.

_____

Form 5–2

AGREEMENT FORM
VOCATIONAL TRAINING CENTER

_____ HIGH SCHOOL

Name _____ D/B _____ Grade _____

Address _____ City _____ Zip _____

Parent or Guardian _____ Phone _____

Term of Contract: From _____ To _____

1. Reason for enrolling _____

    _____

2.   The objectives are: To learn job readiness skills, to study math and English, to complete a variety of job assignments related to industry and personal life enrichment, and to earn credits toward high school graduation or equivalency.

STUDENT AGREES:

    To pursue the prescribed program of study toward the successful completion of program goals by attending two periods of academic study and two periods of vocational training center study.

PARENTS OR GUARDIANS AGREE:

1. To verify the hours reported on the weekly homework log.
2. To maintain contact with the center concerning the student's progress.

SCHOOL DISTRICT AGREES:

1. To provide assistance and guidance to the student.
2. To evaluate the student's work according to procedures of the district and award credit as merited.

    It is understood that this Agreement expires at the end of the current semester. Permission to continue in the program for the next semester will be granted only by permission of instructor.

STUDENTS MAY BE REMOVED FROM THE PROGRAM FOR:

1. Failing to perform assigned work.
2. Not benefiting from the program.
3. Being habitually tardy or absent.
4. Behaving improperly.

_____   _____
(Student's Signature)   (Parent/Guardian's Signature)

_____   _____
(Staff Member's Signature)   (Counselor's Signature)

Form 5–3

VOCATIONAL TRAINING CENTER

Suggested List for Work Stations

1. Accounting & Bookkeeping
2. Advertising
3. Art
4. Auto Body Repair
5. Banking & Credit
6. Bricklaying
7. Carpentry
8. Cleaning & Maintenance
9. Computer Programming
10. Disc Brake Repair
11. Drafting
12. Electrical Work
13. Electric Motor Repair
14. Electronic Assembly
15. Filing
16. Floral Design
17. Greenhouse Work
18. Grocery Clerking
19. Hair Care & Styling
20. Machining
21. Mail Handling
22. Medical Records
23. Painting
24. Plumbing
25. Retail Sales
26. Skin & Nail Care
27. Small Engine Repair
28. Time Clock
29. Typing
30. Upholstery
31. Waiting on Tables
32. Wall Covering
33. Welding
34. Word Processing

Form 5—4

How to Implement a Regional Occupational Program That Will Serve as a Medium for Dropout Prevention

Incorrigible students (those who resist correction, change, or reform) will most likely always be a factor within any school district. These obstinates, commonly referred to as deviants, are unable or unwilling to mold their behavior to fit the requirements of an organized public high school. They differ from delinquents in that they usually do not violate the law. Instead, they simply refuse to follow the rules or to conform, and often try to defy the established regime.

WHERE THE DEVIANT STUDENT CAN FIND VOCATIONAL HELP

Although not intended exclusively for incorrigibles, a Regional Occupational Program (ROP) provides an attractive alternative for these, as well as for other students who are behind in school and who face the prospect of not being able to earn a high school diploma. The program is generally housed off campus and serves all students who apply.

For the most part, it caters to those students who are on the verge of dropping out of their own accord and those who are being threatened with indefinite suspension by the school administration. For these, ROP offers

1. Vocational guidance
2. Testing
3. Work practice
4. On-the-job training

THE REGIONAL OCCUPATIONAL PROGRAM DEFINED

The Regional Occupational Program links the school district with local business in an effort to provide top-quality vocational training to youths and adults who need it. It provides a variety of training opportunities that otherwise might not be available to local districts for two reasons:

1. A local school district may not be able to fund the equipment, facilities, and personnel for such a program on its own.
2. The current academic curriculum cannot be adjusted to include vocational training courses, or cannot spare the time and space for such courses.

It is wise for schools that have existing vocational education courses to keep in mind that the courses offered in the ROP supplement but do not replace them. A regional occupational program permits the expansion of vocational education opportunities at a low cost by allowing students to experience on-the-job training in local firms, offices, and factories.

HOW ROP FUNCTIONS TO BRING HIGH-RISK
STUDENTS BACK INTO THE SYSTEM

Generally speaking, it is sometimes difficult for the school district to envision a vocational education program as an aid to dropout prevention or recovery. However, once the district officials realize that *all* persons from high school age through adulthood, whether currently enrolled in a public school or not, are eligible for ROP, they are inclined to view it more favorably. Therefore, in establishing the ROP, it is important to define as eligible "any student or adult individual who expresses an interest in an occupation and has a desire to pursue training, regardless of previous academic history."

In some states, many youngsters find that ROP becomes *their* school, so to speak. This is simply because it is the only form of education to which they can relate.

Another good feature to keep in mind is that anyone enrolled in ROP will be allowed to credit their efforts toward a high school diploma. When a local high school is selected as the "home school" for the ROP participant who is not enrolled in a district high school, it becomes the responsibility of the home school to keep a transcript for the student.

ORGANIZATION AND IMPLEMENTATION OF ROP

Regional educational programs are usually county-operated and offer a joint agreement for participating school districts. When the ROP is initiated by the county it recruits businesses to supply vocational opportunities and provide centralized sites for regularly scheduled instruction. There are also many ROPs that are operated by a single school district or cooperating districts. They hire consultants to review district vocational training needs and contact host contractors in the community who have a business that can fill these needs. The contractor is then asked to link up with the Regional Occupational Program. See also Form 6–2B, Section I. Background for a sample guideline.

Philosophy and Goals Begin with the Governing School Board

All viable programs should begin with a written proposal to the governing school board. In preparing this critical presentation, it is a good idea to slant the philosophy of the program toward dropout prevention. Some of the points to keep in mind are:

1. Recruitment will be community-based, not school-based.
2. Available student population statistics reflect both the *county-wide* dropout population and the currently enrolled *local* student body.
3. Program objectives should be consistent with a dropout prevention philosophy.
4. Program objectives should include special provisions for students with special needs.

It goes without saying that local school boards should also draft written policies and procedures to guide the program's operation. This can be done by an appointed advisory committee, the teachers, the parents, an administrator—or a combination of all. When done by anyone other than the school board, it should be submitted to the board for approval. The policy and procedure draft should incorporate such items as:

1. Definition, rationale, and scope
2. Procedures for implementation
3. A statement showing the need for the program
4. Organizational and facility changes that may be required, such as building modifications or additions
5. Budget and staff needs
6. Identification of cooperating agents
7. The curriculum to be implemented

See Form 6–1 for a sample guideline.

HINTS ON FUNDING A ROP

Legislation authorizing funds to establish optional specialized secondary programs such as ROP very likely already exists in your state. To find out more about it, acquire the information circular, pamphlet, or other literature issued by the state. This will furnish complete instructions for the compilation and presentation of a proposal by which said funds can be requested. In the unlikely event that your state has no current legislation appropriating funds for new programs, consult Chapter 13 of this text for the steps a school district may take to initiate such legislation. Check your state's educational funding sources through the office of the superintendent of schools in your district. All pertinent information should be available there. If it isn't handy, put in a formal request for it.

DEVELOPING CURRICULUM

To justify the vocational courses that will be offered, it is strongly recommended that the ROP director conduct a job market survey and complete a comprehensive job market analysis for each course. The curriculum will be successful only if there is a demand for the type of job the graduate has been trained to perform.

The most effective plan is to make a written statement of the required curriculum for each course, together with an introductory declaration that contains the following points:

1. A definition of the job to be taught
2. A statement of class goals and objectives

3. An outline of job skills to be learned

4. A statement of any required prerequisites

A copy of the recommended curriculum should be kept on file at a central location. (For a sample of the format, refer to Forms 6–2 A & B.)

STAFFING THE ROP

One program director should be hired for each high school or center operating a ROP. This individual should function as a liaison between the community ROP job site and the students. The director's job includes

1. Spending the necessary time within the community recruiting both large and small businesses and industries that will offer ROP participants on-the-job training

2. Working closely with these local businesses, doing follow-up surveys, and checking student behavior and progress

3. Working up participant evaluation statistics that chart student progress toward developing the necessary work habits, attitudes, and job skills that will enhance their eventual transition into the world of work

It is important to keep in mind that the employer's input is not only essential but will have a strong impact on such findings.

Teachers who work in ROPs are frequently full-time high school educators who teach vocational courses on a part-time basis. This helps to ensure that every class is taught or supervised by a credentialed person. Where accredited teachers are not actually teaching, skilled laymen are contracted to instruct in their particular field of expertise. A dental assistant might be engaged to teach dental hygiene skills or a construction worker to teach certain aspects of carpentry. However, the weekly progress of the student is always evaluated and overseen by a credentialed educator.

INSURANCE

It is normal practice for the county in which the ROP center operates to assume the expense of workers' compensation insurance.

The insurance provides a comfort-level zone to the employers while at the same time eliminating the burden of liability suits. Every ROP employer should be required to execute a contract with the county stating the provisions of the insurance policy and the employer's intent to remain with the program for at least one semester.

An optional enticement to employers is an offer by the county to reimburse employers for losses from theft or damage committed by students during the class sessions.

For a sample county/employer contract, refer to Form 6–3.

SOLVING RECURRING ENROLLMENT PROBLEMS

A program such as a Regional Occupational Program cannot flourish unless possible candidates are aware of its existence. The following three methods have proven to be effective ways of finding and stimulating enrollment, especially among potential and actual dropouts:

1. Have the ROP recruiter call on local high schools in the district.
2. Print information flyers about the program and distribute them in the community or area served by the newly established ROP.
3. Advertise the program in the local newspaper, on television, and on radio.

In all instances, the message should emphasize that *anyone* in the served district who has dropped out of school can use ROP to pick up where he or she left off and further his or her vocational skills.

It is normal for some interested candidates to be reluctant to enroll because of self-determined insurmountable personal problems. However if hesitant candidates are informed that ROP offers *special services* for *special needs*, their self-imposed barriers often disappear and they are enticed to enroll. Most of these problems are minor ones that can easily be solved by the system if it is given a chance. Experience has shown that the two major stumbling blocks are transportation and child care. Solutions to these and other problems can be built into ROP at its inception. The following are typical candidate problems that tend to inhibit candidate enrollment, together with their ROP solutions.

Problem: In regular school, the candidate failed or did poorly in language arts and math.

Solution: As a special service, ROP offers small group tutoring classes in verbal expression and math.

Problem: The hesitant candidate does not own a car, cannot afford gasoline, or cannot afford commercial bus fares.

Solution: As a special service, ROP will pay a percentage of the cost if students provide their own transportation or will supply free bus passes for the local transit system.

Problem: Candidate has a small child to care for.

Solution: As a special service, ROP will set up child care services, using the facilities of an accredited local nursery or preschool day care establishment.

It must be understood that despite the seemingly wide latitude of services ROP offers candidates, certain controls are necessarily practiced. While not discouragingly stringent, they focus attention on eligibility criteria. First, the director meets with the candidate to verify his or her qualifications for the course selected and to determine that all prerequisites have been fulfilled. Second, the candidate is required to fill out and submit an enrollment form. Once enrolled, the candidate is sent information regarding the location and starting date for the first class. (For a sample, refer to Form 6–4.)

Most ROPs use a screening process to help young people acquire an awareness of their own capabilities. This helps them in choosing the most beneficial job experience. The ROP offers the same wide range of training opportunities as those listed in Chapter 5. (Refer to Form 5–4.)

One testing service that is in popular use in ROPs in California is the Career Ability Placement Survey. Often referred to as CAPS, it is published and issued by Educational and Industrial Testing Service, San Diego, California. The CAPS consists of a series of tests that demonstrate potentials, strengths, and weaknesses. Thus it gives some suggestion of the success one may expect in pursuing various career activities. Abilities that are measured include the following:

1. Mechanical aptitude

2. Reasoning power

3. Language usage

4. Manual speed

5. Dexterity

Since students score their own tests, it becomes immediately apparent to them that there are jobs, or even groups of jobs, for which they have measurable aptitude and in which they can expect a high level of career success.

Other possible test choices include an interest inventory that shows the type of work the student may be attracted to and a personal inventory that shows whether a student's temperament and character are suited to a particular career.

ROP is considered a success when the student who graduates from the program has developed the necessary skills to obtain a satisfying job, sustain a pleasing life, and become a productive member of society. In addition, many students develop an increased self-understanding and decision-making skills that will increase their likelihood of success in the world of work.

When a youngster acquires these competencies and abilities, the high school diploma in itself does not loom quite so large as an essential part of a bright future. The term, *high school dropout*, loses much of its stigma when the student can show a Certificate of Accomplishment (or the equivalent) when applying for a job.

The following case history will serve to illustrate how ROP helped an unruly, arrogant, and egotistical youngster to become a "graduate." Although the student did not earn a high school diploma, her vocational skills improved to a degree that enabled her to acquire a license and support herself through gainful employment. She is no longer considered a high school dropout.

CASE HISTORY OF BONNIE: AN INCORRIGIBLE STUDENT

Bonnie was a loud youngster with very dark hair and eyes to match. Her cosmetic appearance was not helped by inky, pencil-lined eyebrows, large false eyelashes, bright red lipstick, and a well-defined spot of very pink rouge on each cheek. She was well-endowed and had a tendency to wear clothing that revealed rather than concealed. She appeared much older than her eighteen years, and labored under the delusion that she already knew everything there was to know. She considered continuing her education a waste of time.

In eight school semesters, Bonnie had actually passed only one course out of forty. The paperwork in her file was so confusing that three different birth dates had been recorded for her. Five surnames were recorded for each of her parents, and her address was listed as a city in South America—her mother's birthplace. It was nearly impossible to decipher Bonnie's exact status. Bonnie herself insisted she needed to finish only one or two more classes to complete her eligibility for graduation.

Breaking Down the Barriers of Reception Resistance

It is common knowledge among educators that it is difficult to convince, inspire, or coerce students like Bonnie to do anything they feel is of no special benefit to them, especially if it is a new idea. Communication with such students is a frustrating exercise, since they generally refuse to listen. Often, it seems as if they have no "in going wires," or no antenna with which to receive and comprehend someone else's ideas. The counselor's first step, then, is to find some way to get a message across, directly or indirectly.

One good way to start is to talk about something in which the student is obviously deeply interested.

Judging by the way Bonnie dressed and used makeup, it was a safe bet she considered herself highly fashionable. Her counselor decided to ask her a question about her long, red, manicured fingernails, as if she were soliciting advice from Bonnie and would be grateful for her expert contribution. Bonnie brightened at the question and responded with an eloquent step-by-step depiction of the methods and practices used to achieve the ultimate in nail care.

The educator who asks the right question may be astonished to learn how well versed a student can be in subjects that are completely unrelated to academics. At this point it is a good idea to reinforce the student's enthusiasm by suggesting in a sincere manner that a person possessing this kind of talent has the potential to earn a substantial salary by offering it as a service to other people.

This is usually the turning point. The student's eyes or expression may betray an inner conflict as the need for appreciation battles with the deep-seated incorrigibility. If there is any hope at all for the student's salvation, this is the moment when it has a chance to be fulfilled. In Bonnie's case, after what seemed like an enormous length of time, and some eye searching, she responded.

"You mean . . . me? A manicurist?" she said hesitantly.

The best kind of answer is a simple "Yes," or "Of course." Anything more elaborate might jeopardize the student's willingness to listen.

Having gone this far, the student will usually ask how this can be accomplished. Once the student is responding and a dialogue has been established, you know that the barriers to communication have been lowered. Now is the time to explain the opportunities offered by the regional occupational program *in the student's field of interest*.

Bending the Rules Can Mean the Difference Between Success and Failure

It is too much to expect, however, that the entire problem can be solved so easily. When placing any incorrigible child, such as Bonnie, in a tightly controlled and structured environment, there is bound to be some initial conflict.

First, Bonnie rebelled against the nine-to-five workday. But because ROP is flexible, the administrators solved the problem by adjusting her work period so she could sleep late.

Next, she challenged the study of nutrition, chemistry, and other subjects she felt did not pertain to nail grooming. One confrontation followed another. On more than one occasion she walked out of class, failed to appear for important tests, and argued with her teachers. Only the latitude permitted in ROP and the patience and dedication of her instructors kept her in school. Kicking her out of the program would not have accomplished anything beneficial for Bonnie. It would only have added to her already long list of failures, and her self-image would have deteriorated further.

It took Bonnie thirty-six weeks to complete the program. This was three times the usual time. But as long as she was willing, the teachers strove with her. On the day she "graduated," she was as arrogant as ever. It was difficult to understand the motivating force that drove her. It seems unlikely that she completed the course to please the system's personnel; it is more likely that she did it to prove to the world that she could indeed "graduate" without a high school diploma. The fact remains that ROP was an inspiration and an incentive toward final success.

While ROP was instrumental in preventing Bonnie from dropping out and was able to provide her with tangible evidence of accomplishment in the form of a course certificate, Bonnie was still not interested in completing the classes required to earn a high school diploma. Yet the records show that many other youngsters, relying on the credits earned in ROP, have gone on to do exactly that, finally winning that coveted high school diploma and attaining a goal that had long seemed out of reach.

BOARD POLICY

UNION HIGH SCHOOL DISTRICT

Guidelines for Implementing Regional Occupational Programs

I. Definition, Rationale, Scope

A. *Definition:* The Regional Occupational Program endeavors to link the school district with local businesses in an effort to provide vocational training to youths.

B. *Rationale:* There are times when it is in a student's best interest to include vocational education in his or her program, in addition to, or instead of, regular course requirements. Schoolwork seems more relevant when it is related to future, long-range employment. Students are less likely to drop out of school when involved in a work program.

C. Any individual (from high school enrollment age upward) who expresses an interest in an occupation, and has a desire to pursue further training, regardless of previous academic history, is eligible for this program. The educational goal of the student may range from completing a single job-training course to fulfillment of diploma requirements.

II. Procedures for Implementation of a Regional Occupational Program

A. *Supervision:* Each school shall designate a certified person to act as liaison between job sites and students. This coordinator shall be responsible for overseeing the functioning of the program.

B. *Coordination:* Each school shall develop guidelines for:
   1. Identifying students who are candidates for the program
   2. Enrolling students in the program
   3. Monitoring student progress
   4. Evaluating student learning.

III. Goals and Objectives of a Regional Occupational Program

A. To develop responsible work habits and attitudes necessary for making a successful transition to the world of work

B. To develop skills necessary to obtain a satisfying job, sustain a pleasing lifestyle, and become a productive member of society

C. To increase self-understanding and decision-making skills

D. To provide students with hands-on experience in a variety of jobs

E. To expose students to specialized training in entry-level jobs

F. To remediate student weaknesses as identified by the job-site supervisor

G. To provide structured contacts between students and vocational training site supervisors to ensure a successful work experience.

IV. Records

Adequate records shall be maintained at a central site and shall include but not be limited to

A. A copy of this board policy statement

B. A list of students (past and present) who have participated in the Regional Occupational Program together with the appropriate paperwork

C. A grading system for evaluation and progress

V. Funding

Regional Occupational Programs are reimbursed per student based on an average daily attendance of _____ days or _____ hours.

Form 6–1

BERGEN COUNTY OFFICE OF EDUCATION

Address	City	State	Zip

TO: Date: _____

FROM:

SUBJECT: PROSPECTUS FORMAT FOR NEW AND EXPANDING ROP PROGRAMS

The following prospectus will be used to present new and/or expanding ROP programs to the ROP Steering Committee, ROP Administration, and Superintendent's Cabinet. The prospectus is to be completed at least three weeks before the next meeting of the ROP Steering Committee.

The format is as follows:

   I.   Need Statement and Background
  II.   Program Goal
 III.   Job Market Analysis
     a.   Jobs (list Department of Transportation phone number)
     b.   Job market projections
     c.   Career ladder
 IV.   Technical Advisory Support (minutes attached)
  V.   Program Operation
     a.   Instruction individually contracted or County Office of Education, teacher, etc.)
     b.   Enrollment, location, time
     c.   Facilities and equipment
     d.   Transportation
     e.   Ancillary services
        (1)   Counseling and guidance
        (2)   Job Placement
     f.   Business/industry involvement (community classroom)
 VI   Course outline
VII.   Budget

Form 6–2A

COURSE PROSPECTUS

BERGEN REGIONAL OCCUPATION PROGRAM

TITLE: OFFICE OCCUPATIONS: WORD PROCESSING

Starting Date: _____   Current Date: _____

Contracted _____ With Whom _____ (host contractor name) _____

General _____

A.M. _____ P.M. _____

New _____   _____

                      Area Coordinator

                      Semester length   1   2   3   4
                                           (circle)

                      Total Hours _____ Daily Hours _____

                      Sections   1   2   3   4
                                       (circle)

I. BACKGROUND

In March of 1987, the (school or district name) ROP hired a group of consultants to review their vocational training programs. In the final report of this study it was suggested that (host contractor name) could upgrade their own vocational training programs by linking up with the (school or district name) Regional Occupational Program. As a result of this recommendation, (host contractor name) requested that the ROP develop courses that would include their training program.

After reviewing the report, ROP staff decided to develop two or three model programs that would successfully accomplish this goal. In addition, (host contractor name) requested that classroom instruction be offered on their premises and that (school or district name) students be allowed to utilize the community classroom sites for training.

This proposal requests approval to implement a word processing class.

II. PROGRAM GOAL

Individuals will be prepared for entry-level employment in clerical positions in automated word and data processing.

III. PROGRAM DESCRIPTION

This is a two-semester class in which students acquire a basic under-standing of word processing and learn to operate various types of word processing equipment. When they have attained an adequate skill level, students will be placed at a local business site for appropriate training four days each week.

Students will be trained for jobs as word processing technicians, key-data entry operators, data processors, secretaries, or clerk-typists. Students will gain experience in office organization and operations, personnel policies and requirements, and the use of automatic office equipment. They will be trained in letter writing, machine dictation, and transcription.

IV. JOB MARKET ANALYSIS

Workers in this occupational group perform a wide range of tasks needed to keep businesses and other organizations running on a day-to-day basis. These tasks included activities such as preparing, transcribing, systematizing, and preserving written communications and records; distributing information; and collecting accounts.

According to State Projections of Employment by Industry and Occupation for 1980–1990 and State Employment Development Department and Employment Data Research Division, in 1980, clerical workers were estimated to be the single largest occupational group in the state, with over 2.2 million job holders. The increasing volume of paperwork and record keeping, the growing complexity of large corporations, and the industry growth will allow clerical occupations to reflect healthy growth between 1980 and 1990, with the total number of clerical workers exceeding 2.8 million by 1990, nearly one-quarter of all projected jobs in the state. Clerical employment is concentrated in a few specific occupations, including secretaries, bookkeepers, general clerks, cashiers, and typists. Secretaries are expected to show the largest employment growth of the occupation in this state, adding 116,300 new jobs in the ten-year period, for an increase of 43 percent. General clerks will show the third largest gain, with a projected 70,000 new jobs, and cashiers will be sixth, with 54,000 new jobs."

V. PROGRAM OPERATION INFORMATION

A. *Enrollment*

Approximately twelve students will be trained. The classroom facility will be located at the (host contractor name) job center. The program will be open to (host contractor name) trainees as well as twelfth-grade students from local high schools, plus adults and out-of-school youths.

B. *Instruction*

The (name of your state) County Office of Education will each school day, provide one half day of service by properly credentialed vocational instructors. Costs for the instructor will include all charges for salary, fringe benefits, transportation costs (when needed), and any authorized in-service costs.

All student instruction and training will be provided for and supervised by the certified teacher, who will be an employee of (name of your state) County Office of Education. A technical advisory committee representing the industry will annually review the curriculum and make recommendations for change if deemed necessary.

Teaching strategies will include simulation activities, field experience, field trips, guest speakers, displays, comparison testing, and demonstrations.

C. *Curriculum Development*

The curriculum for this course has been developed by the instructor, personnel of (host contractor), the ROP, and an ad hoc committee from the field. The instructor will establish a student training plan for each field training site. The plan will identify the areas of skilled training to be provided and the approximate number of hours that training will be provided in each of the skill areas.

D. *Advisory Committee Recommendations*

An advisory committee has met and recommended approval for this program. Please see the attached minutes.

E. *Business/Industry Involvement*

An integral part of this program is student involvement in training at business/industry sites. ROP trainees will not be permitted to replace work experience students.

F. *Facilities, Equipment, and Instructional Materials*

The (host contractor) will provide a teaching classroom. Supplies, material, books, and equipment in the dollar amounts detailed in the budget will be provided by the _____ County Office of Education Regional Occupational Program.

G. *Ancillary Services*

(1) Transportation

The (host contractor) will provide transportation for their students from the (host contractor) job center to their training station and back.

(2) Counseling and Guidance

Career guidance and counseling will be provided by (host contractor) staff.

(3) Job Placement

All individuals satisfactorily completing this class will be provided placement services, including job information and training in job-seeking skills.

(4) Other

Additional services provided to ROP enrollees include workers' compensation and medical coverage.

VI. CAREER OPPORTUNITIES

Career opportunities exist in the following areas:

Titles	*Department of Transportation Number*
Data Entry	203.582-030
Clerk Typist	203.362-010
Data Entry (Clerical)	203.582-030
Secretary	201.362-030
Typist	203.588-122
Office Machine Operator	207.682-010
Word Processor	203.362-022
Terminal System Operator	203.362-018
Transcribing Machine Operator	203.582-058

VII. COURSE OUTLINE

A. PRETESTS/POSTTESTS: 12 HOURS

1. Typing—speed and accuracy

2. Formatting—business documents placement
3. Basic Skills—business math, spelling, vocabulary, grammar, punctuation, capitalization, number expression, proofreading, composition
4. Employment readiness—Job aptitudes and attitudes, job application and interview skills

B. WORD PROCESSING AND DATA ENTRY CAREER PATHS: <u>45 HOURS</u>
1. Origin of word processing
2. Word processing as a system
3. Applications
4. Careers in word and information processing

C. GROOMING: <u>10 HOURS</u>
1. Personal Appearance
2. Clothes for the job
3. Makeup

D. EMPLOYMENT RELATED COMPETENCIES: <u>16 HOURS</u>
1. Basic skills (math and language)
2. Following instructions

E. SUPPLEMENTAL OFFICE SKILLS (if not already learned):   <u>30 HOURS</u>
1. Filing
2. Ten-key calculator by touch
3. Telephone techniques

F. TYPING SKILLS: <u>45 HOURS</u>
1. Speed and accuracy
2. Standard formatting
3. Proofreading
4. Composition
5. Statistical typing
6. Machine transcription

G. WORD PROCESSING AND DATA ENTRY SKILLS: <u>85 HOURS</u>
1. Development of operator skills on various word processing and data entry hardware and using various software packages
2. Document, manuscript, and business letter production
3. Individualized learning plans and performance evaluations
4. Job training site placement for qualified students

H. JOB-SEEKING SKILLS   <u>10 HOURS</u>
1. Job applications
2. Interview techniques
3. Resume preparation
4. Job readiness

I. REMEDIATION: AS NEEDED
As determined by evaluation of ongoing performance

J. INTERNSHIP: <u>235 HOURS</u>

TOTAL HOURS   <u>540 HOURS</u>

Form 6–2B

REGIONAL OCCUPATIONAL PROGRAM
JOINT VENTURE AGREEMENT

THIS AGREEMENT is entered into this _____ day of, _____ by and between _____ County Office of Education, Regional Educational Program (name) (ROP), hereinafter referred to as "County," and_____
_____ ,
(address)

hereinafter referred to as "Company."

WITNESSETH:

WHEREAS Company desires to provide for the instruction of students to gain employment skills by means of program of on-site training; and

WHEREAS Company is sympathetic to the educational objectives of providing training for the students of the County;

NOW THEREFORE IT IS HEREBY AGREED AS FOLLOWS:

1. Company will provide training stations that will provide for these students (furnished by the County) who are eligible to participate in the training program and who are qualified and acceptable to Company as determined by its PERSONNEL MANAGER the opportunity to expand the competencies developed in the classroom instruction portion of their training.

2. Company may reject students who are not qualified or are otherwise not acceptable and may decline to train any student when it determines at any time that no suitable training station is available.

3. Company may terminate the training of any student who does not perform satisfactorily or if company determines at any time that no suitable training station is available. Company will advise County prior to taking such actions.

4. Company *shall not compensate students* for any activities related to the ROP training provided hereunder, and students performing training activities for the Company hereunder shall not be considered employees of Company.

5. County, pursuant to the provisions of Education Code Section _____, agrees to secure, upon written request, a Certificate of Insurance showing public liability and property damage insurance for the County limits of ONE HUNDRED THOUSAND DOLLARS ($100,000.00) for one person injured in one accident and THREE HUNDRED THOUSAND DOLLARS ($300,000.00) for any one occurrence regardless of number of persons injured, and TEN THOUSAND DOLLARS ($10,000.00) property damage for any one occurrence.

6. The _____ County Office of Education will provide coverage under the policies of school's Insurance Authority for Liability and Workers' Compensation Liability for medical benefits for students during the training activities.

7. County shall hold harmless the Company, its officers, agents, and employees for any claims for damages or loss, and any claim for wages, benefits, or other compensation resulting from the acts of omission of County, its officers, agents, employees, and students with respect to the program.

8. County shall:
   a. Assign students performing training activities hereunder to training stations providing experience consistent with the purpose of the training program.
   b. Instruct students as to Company's rules and regulations to be adhered to while they are performing training activities hereunder.
   c. In cooperation with Company, provide a written plan of training activities for each individual student placed in training with the Company which insures that said student may realize maximum training benefits.
   d. Verify that the training activities set forth in each individual student's plan of training are in an occupation for which there is local demand.
   e. Make suggestions on training site safety to see that the requirements of the law are met and health, safety, and welfare of students is not endangered.

9. Company shall:
   a. Provide County with a written performance rating on each student performing training activities hereunder. Said performance rating shall be accomplished on forms furnished to Company by County.
   b. Consult the County instructor-supervisor assigned to each student regarding problems which may arise pertaining to student's training performance and behavior.
   c. Permit the County instructor-supervisor of each student to observe the student while performing training activities hereunder.
   d. Maintain accurate records of student's attendance at the training station.

10. Company shall not utilize the services of any student whom it is training under this Agreement to displace or replace any Company employee, to impair existing contracts for service, or to fill any vacant position.

11. No student shall be denied participation in the Regional Occupational Program either by County or Company because of race, age, color, religion, sex, national origin, or handicap.

12. All laws or rules applicable to minors in employment relationships are applicable to students participating in the training program under this Agreement.

Either party may terminate this Agreement upon delivering to the other party thirty (30) days' written notice of intent to terminate. Notwithstanding such termination, this Agreement may remain in full force and effect as long as assigned students are performing training activities.

IN WITNESS WHEREOF, the parties hereto have executed this Agreement as of the day and year first above written.

_____
Superintendent

_____ County Schools

By: _____
    Assistant Superintendant

_____ (Company Name) _____

_____ (Street) _____

_____ (City and Zip Code) _____

By: _____ (Signature) _____

         "COUNTY"   "COMPANY"

Approved by County Board of
Education in regular meeting
held _____.

Approved as to form by counsel.

_____
_____

FOR ROP INSTRUCTOR'S USE ONLY (Instructor must complete the following information) _____

ROP INSTRUCTOR INFORMATION

COMPANY CONTACT INFORMATION

ROP Course
Title: _____

ROP Intructor: _____
_____

Phone: _____

Company
Contact name: _____

Department: _____
_____

Phone: _____

Form 6–3

APPLICATION FOR ENROLLMENT
UNION VOCATIONAL EDUCATION

[ ] ROP   [ ] Fall
[ ] New Enrollment   [ ] Spring YEAR 19 ____

[ ] _____   [ ] Summer

[ ] Change From: _____

NAME: (Print) _____
                    Last   First   Initial

ADDRESS: _____
               Number   Street   Zip

_____ PHONE: _____

ROP COURSE DESIRED   1. _____ [ ] A.M.   [ ] P.M.

                     2. _____ [ ] A.M.   [ ] P.M.

SCHOOL YR. (at time of entering course)   [ ] Soph. [ ] Jr. [ ] Sr.

DATE OF H.S. GRADUATION (if graduated)   [ ] Jan.   [ ] June 19 ____

HIGH SCHOOL _____ Career/W.E. Coord. _____

DATE OF BIRTH _____ AGE _____

SOCIAL SECURITY NUMBER _____/_____/_____

NAME OF PARENT OR GUARDIAN: _____

                 PHONE: (___) ____ - _____

I can provide my own transportation if necessary: [ ] Yes [ ] No

PARENT'S (Guardian's) SIGNATURE: _____

                 DATE: _____

STUDENT'S SIGNATURE: _____

                 DATE: _____

Student Accepted: Yes [ ] No [ ]   By: _____

                 Title: _____

                 Date: _____

Form 6–4

WORK EXPERIENCE EDUCATION
UNION UNIFIED SCHOOL DISTRICT

RETURN TO: Career Work Experience Education Coordinator

STUDENT'S WORK RECORD

STUDENT'S NAME: _____

EMPLOYER'S NAME: _____
(Business or Firm)

COORDINATOR'S NAME: _____

SUPERVISOR'S NAME: _____

MONTHLY WORK SCHEDULE

TO EMPLOYERS: For students to receive the maximum number of credits from W.E.E., they *must work an average of 15 hours per week and no less than three school days.*

Month	Total Hourse Worked Each Week			
September	(1)	(2)	(3)	(4)
October	(1)	(2)	(3)	(4)
November	(1)	(2)	(3)	(4)
December	(1)	(2)	(3) Christmas	(4) Vacation
January	(1)	(2)	(3)	(4)
February	(1)	(2)	(3)	(4)
March	(1)	(2)	(3)	(4)
April	(1)	(2)	(3)	(4)
May	(1)	(2)	(3)	(4)
June	(1)	(2)		

The hours listed above are correct and can be verified by the student's/employee's payroll records.

_____   _____
(Employer's signature)   (Date)

Final signature of employer required upon completion of the program.

Form 6–5

ACCEPTANCE INTO PROGRAM

STUDENT'S NAME: _____

CONGRATULATIONS!

You have been accepted for enrollment in the _____ course of the Regional Occupational Program (ROP).

The course will begin _____(date)_____
Information you need to know is as follows:

Time: _____ Teacher's Name: _____

Location: _____ Room Number: _____

Program Phone No.: _____

Bus transportation is available as indicated below:

	BUS No.	LEAVES	ARRIVES	LOCATION
_____ to ROP	_____	_____	_____	_____
Transfer to Bus	_____	_____	_____	_____
Return to _____	_____	_____	_____	_____
Transfer to Bus	_____	_____	_____	_____

At the beginning of the semester the bus schedule may vary slightly from that stated above. Familiarize yourself with the bus driver and with pickup and drop-off locations. Don't get discouraged—check with the undersigned or your school counselor if you have any problems.

Here are a few guidelines that will contribute to your success in your course with ROP.

*ATTENDANCE: *Daily* attendance, in the classroom and/or the training site, is required.

*FURLOUGHS: If you go on furlough—even for one week—you must continue to go to your ROP class during your furlough period.

*SMOKING: Smoking is *not* allowed on the bus or at the pickup and drop-off sites.

*LUNCH: May be eaten on the ROP bus. You are required to clean up any mess you may have made while eating.

_____
(Coordinator)

Phone: _____

Form 6–6

VOCATIONAL EDUCATION—ACCEPTANCE INTO PROGRAM
YORK UNIFIED SCHOOL DISTRICT

STUDENT'S NAME: _____

ROOM NUMBER: _____

PERIOD: _____

CONGRATULATIONS !!!!!!!!

  You have been accepted for enrollment in the following ROP occupational

preparation program: _____ .

ROP _____ _____ during the A.M. _____ P.M. _____ .

session for periods: 1 2 3 4 5 6 7 8. This program is to be held

at _____ . Transportation will _____ /will

not _____ be provided.

  Please notify me if there is any change in your plans. We have a waiting list of
interested students.

_____

Coordinator

Date: _____

Form 6–7

STUDENT INTEREST INTERVIEW

Name: _____ Date _____

Age: _____ Grade: _____ R _____ S _____

1. What kind of things do you do in your spare time in the:
   (a) Afternoons after school? Where do you usually go?
   (b) Nights and evenings?
   (c) Summers? This past summer?

2. With whom do you usually spend your free time?
   (a) No one _____
   (b) Family _____
   (c) One friend _____
   (d) Group of friends _____ same age _____ older _____ younger _____

3. What was the happiest school year you ever had? What about the least happiest year? What do you remember about the year that made you happy/unhappy? Explain briefly:

4. What is your favorite:
   (a) Kind of music?   _____
   (b) Radio station?   _____
   (c) Kind of thing to read?   _____
   (d) Type of movie?   _____
   (e) Sport to watch?   _____
   (f) Sport to play?   _____
   (g) Hobby?   _____
   (h) Have you ever played on a team?   [ ] Yes   [ ] No

5. List some things you really do well: _____
   _____

6. Do you belong to any clubs at school, church, camp? _____
   Name them: _____

7. Do you have a part-time job now? Yes _____ No _____   If yes,
   where? _____

   How did you get it?
   (a) On my own   [ ]
   (b) Someone I know helped me get it   [ ]
   (c) Other _____

8. Name all the kinds of jobs you have ever done, and tell which jobs you liked and which you got paid for:

Jobs you have done	Paid For	Liked
_____	_____	_____
_____	_____	_____
_____	_____	_____
_____	_____	_____

9. Which job did you like the best? _____
    Why? _____
10. Which job did you like the least? _____
    Why? _____
11. Do you want to stay in this area when you graduate? _____
12. After you graduate from high school, what kind of job would you like to have?
    Name three or four.
    1. _____   3. _____
    2. _____   4. _____
13. Do you qualify for any of these jobs now?   [ ] Yes   [ ] No
    Do you know the qualifications necessary to obtain these jobs?
    [ ] Yes   [ ] No
    If so, what are they? _____

    _____

14. Do you think you know enough about different jobs to make a choice now, or
    do you think you need to investigate the duties, pay, hours, and training
    necessary for the jobs you're interested in?
        Know enough [ ]   Need to investigate [ ]
15. Have you ever been to the career center?   [ ] Yes   [ ] No
16. If you were offered a part-time job after school—right now—do you think you
    would know how to work cooperatively with the boss and your fellow workers?
        [ ] Yes   [ ] No
17. Have you ever been through a formal interview?   [ ] Yes   [ ] No
    If so, how did it go? [ ] Pretty good   [ ] Not so good
    What would you do differently for the next interview?

    _____

18. Which of the following would help you get a job?
    [ ] To improve the way I look
    [ ] To improve the way I act with adults and peers
    [ ] To improve my attitude toward work
    [ ] To know what I can and can't do
    [ ] To handle criticism better
    [ ] To practice interviewing
    [ ] To practice filling out application forms
    [ ] To learn to feel better about myself
    [ ] To get some (unpaid) practical work experience
    [ ] To improve my attendance and tardiness
    [ ] To learn to ask for help when I need it
    [ ] To improve my attitude toward school
19. Do you live with your parents?   [ ] Yes   [ ] No
20. Are either of your parents (or guardians) working?
    Father: [ ] Yes   [ ] No   Mother: [ ] Yes   [ ] No
    If yes, explain briefly what kind of job each does.

    _____

    _____

21. Who else is in your family? List by name and age:

22. How do you get along with your parents or guardian?
    [ ]   We enjoy being together
    [ ]   We occasionally have disagreements
    [ ]   We have lots of disagreements
    [ ]   I avoid them as much as possible
    [ ]   My parents do not understand me
    [ ]   My parents listen to me
    [ ]   I listen to my parents
23. Do you talk to anyone about your problems or feelings?
    [ ] Yes   [ ] No
    Do you ever talk to any adults?   [ ] Yes   [ ] No
    Check the persons with whom you talk:
    [ ]   Parents: Mom [ ]   Dad [ ]   Stepfather [ ]   Stepmother [ ]
    [ ]   Guardian or foster parent
    [ ]   Religious leader or spiritual guide
    [ ]   School teacher
    [ ]   Grandparents
    [ ]   Other
    [ ]   None of the above
24. In what situation do you usually find you are the happiest?
    [ ]   At home with my family
    [ ]   At home by myself
    [ ]   At school
    [ ]   Working
    [ ]   When I am with friends
    [ ]   Going places (beach, movies, etc.)
    [ ]   Other
25. Comments:

    _____
    _____
    _____
    _____
    _____

Form 6–8

Making Use of Community Schools to Help At-Risk Youngsters Continue Their Education

Young people who are incarcerated for crimes, or who are pulled from their homes because they are victims of abuse and neglect, are often unnecessarily and unintentionally given the debilitating label of high school dropout. Intervention by well-meaning individuals seeking to protect the child is often successful in generating remedial measures such as counseling, referral to community assistance programs, the filing of criminal charges, or even the removal of the minor from a dangerous environment. Yet little thought is given to the youngster's placement in a suitable substitute learning institution.

On a daily basis, over one million American children are involved in some sort of legal trouble that disrupts not only their lives but their education.

In an effort to protect the youngsters from abuse, or in cases in which incarceration is necessary to protect society itself from the offender, these young people are often torn from a familiar environment and placed into a strange one without much regard for the impact such an action might have on the continuity of their schooling.

Acting in good faith, local communities are apt to set up such assistance agencies and programs as abuse councils and neighborhood retreats, but they are rarely farsighted enough to establish a Community School program designed to prevent troubled youths from becoming dropouts. It is only good sense to see to it that when young people are incarcerated or put under the protective custody of the juvenile court, their schooling does not come to a screeching halt. Responsibility for this matter should be relegated to the county offices of education by the state legislature.

WHAT IS A COMMUNITY SCHOOL PROGRAM?

A Community School Program is an established creative educational institution designed to serve socially disoriented youths with solutions to problems that cannot be dealt with in a traditional school setting. It provides an alternative method of continued learning for youngsters who cannot or do not fit into the regular school system or its alternative programs. This alternative program reclaims and exposes them to a specialized education process. (Programs of this type or nature may have any variety of names. In this text they shall be known as Community School Programs.)

Although similar in curriculum and setup to Opportunity Programs and Continuation Schools, Community School Programs are smaller and have correspondingly small enrollments. They are usually operated by a county board of education in cooperation with the probation department, the Superior Court, and the office of the district attorney.

The functional objectives of a Community School Program generally include the following:

1. To assist students to achieve a high school diploma or GED certificate

2. To teach basic reading, writing, and math skills

3. To assist in the development of marketable job skills

4. To provide an education for incarcerated students and to minimize academic loss while the student is involved in the juvenile justice process

5. To provide a guidance program that helps students develop attitudes more wholesome and rewarding than the ones that brought them into contact with law enforcement authorities

6. To deal with the students' social disorientation and provide a course of readjustment that will allow a quick return to their home school. (Older students, however, may find it desirable to graduate from community school)

THE INITIAL STEP TOWARD IMPLEMENTING A COMMUNITY SCHOOL

Check current state legislation for a bill that allocates funds for the operation of Community Schools by the counties. Such bills usually set the parameters of enrollment, allowing the community schools to accept the following:

1. Pupils who have been expelled from a comprehensive high school or another alternative school

2. Pupils who have been referred to the county by the School Attendance Review Board

3. Pupils who are court wards, or who are on probation from juvenile hall or camps, and who are not in attendance at any school

In addition, the education code will generally also set out guidelines for the manner of enrollment, the length of the school year in days, and some objectives the school is expected to achieve, together with an outline of procedures for their accomplishment.

Along these lines, it is always wise to establish written local policies and procedures for the program. See Board Policy (Form 4–1) Chapter 4.

ENROLLMENT PROCEDURES

To keep the enrollment process orderly, it is a good idea to make use of progressive forms. A student referral and information form should be completed by the referring agency. (See Form 7–1.) Once the referral reaches the Community School personnel, it is carefully screened by a counselor or teacher. This staff member then makes a judgment about the youngster's ability to function in the Community School environment.

Generally, the next step is an interview with the student, sometimes including a parent, guardian, or officer of the court. The main reason for this interview is it allows the school staff to gain some familiarity with the student's personality and to review, for the benefit and edification of all concerned, the operating procedures and rules of the Community School. (See Form 7–2.) During this hearing, the counselor should impress upon the student that an effort is being made to provide an opportunity for completion of his or her interrupted education, as well as for his or her rehabilitation.

Once a student has agreed to participate in the Community School, a school site and a teacher are chosen. It is important that the youngster have good rapport with the teacher. The personnel responsible for the placement should have a thorough knowledge of each teacher and school site. The teacher should be able to set up an educational goal for the student and provide the curriculum needed to complete this goal. Student assessment is a vital part of the Community School program. The more individualized the instruction, the more likely it is that the student will advance academically and that the student will fit in when he or she returns to society. Each student's level of achievement in reading, math, and language skills should be assessed at the time of entry into the school. Remember, these young persons are dropouts. They have left both society and the school system.

It is wise to check your local diploma requirements, as they may differ not only from state to state, but also from district to district and from county to county. It is a good idea to define specifically the authorization under which the Community School diploma will be issued, in order to guide students toward the correct educational goal. The requirements for graduation from a Community School program should be clearly stated in the board policy. Guidelines for evaluating transcripts and setting goals for students can be incorporated in a form designed for that purpose. (See Form 7–3.)

Other forms are also instrumental in ensuring the smooth functioning of the operation and programs. The board policy reiterates the education code, provides guidelines for enrollment, and sets forth referral procedures and diploma requirements. A copy of this policy should be kept at all program sites. Procedures for dropping students from the programs must be clearly outlined and documented. A letter should be sent to the home of the student and to the referring agency. (See Form 7–4.)

Regular progress reports on students are a boon to auditing and recordkeeping. It has been found that those schools which keep up-to-date progress reports are generally the most successful because the reports serve as a motivation for goal accomplishment. (See Form 7–5.)

STAFFING COMMUNITY SCHOOLS

Past experience with community schools demonstrates that inexperienced first-year teachers do not function well in them. It is preferable to engage teachers who have had four or more years in a traditional classroom and have acquired some expertise in dealing with troubled youth. It is even more preferable to seek teachers who have experience in alternative education programs and who have a counseling background. The young people in a Community School generally need as much counseling as they do teaching.

The bulk of enrollments in community schools generally consists of students who have extreme discipline problems. These are youngsters who are on probation or who have been adjudicated wards of the court for committing a crime. This type of adolescent generally is better off in a special environment in which he can continue his education. Some of these students are simply too disruptive, while others have tendencies toward such violent acts as rape and murder. Placement of these latter types in a traditional educational setting would, of course, be a threat to the well-being of the other students, as well as to teachers and staff members.

Some youths who have been declared wards of the court have committed only the so-called "status" offenses—for example, chronic truancy, disobeying their parents or other authorities, and running away from home. The Community School Programs should be designed to fit the needs of those who

1. Have been expelled or excluded from other school programs
2. Are chronic truants or dropouts
3. Are considered "at-risk" youths by the county's juvenile system, county welfare department, or other referring agency, such as:
   a. School districts (expelled students)
   b. Private schools (expelled students)
   c. County Superior Court (wards of court)
   d. County probation department
   e. School Attendance Review Board
   f. Other public and private community agencies, including group homes

FINDING THE PROPER SITE AND CORRECT HOUSING

It is desirable to have more than one Community School so that students can be grouped according to the seriousness of their offenses. Youngsters who have committed violent crimes should be segregated from those who are merely "status" offenders. Possible Community School sites include the following:

1. A school located within the confines of the county juvenile hall for students who have committed serious crimes and are being detained by juvenile court. This school should offer these special programs:
   a. Remedial work for students with deficiencies in language arts, reading, and mathematics
   b. A transcript evaluation service
   c. Special education diagnostic and instructional service
   d. A General Education Development testing center
   e. A diploma-oriented program for older students
2. A school located near the juvenile hall facility for students who are no longer incarcerated. This school should
   a. Offer rehabilitation in cooperation with the probation department
   b. Aim to help students develop self-understanding and adjust to acceptable roles in society

  c. Help students develop positive attitudes toward themselves and society
  d. Build students' confidence in their individual capabilities academically, vocationally, and emotionally
3. A "neighborhood center" school for students who are "status" offenders. The school would
  a. Keep students up-to-date in their current classes and assignments so that they can achieve a smooth transition back to a comprehensive school program
  b. Offer a diploma program for older students
  c. Offer an intensive counseling program for every student

In seeking a site for the neighborhood center, it is important to keep in mind that the center's work requirements and expectations for achievement are very similar to those of regular junior and senior high schools and that the school environment is a factor in students' progress. The school itself can play a unique part in the rehabilitation of the offending student, provided the center is wisely located. If, for instance, commercial businesses and industrial operations are the center's next-door neighbors, students may have the opportunity to observe business practices and production techniques, and possibly to acquire part-time jobs.

Practical application has shown that the following sites are ideal for such experiences:

1. A storefront or shopping-center location close to a variety of businesses
2. An old campus, closed by the district, that is situated in an area that is undergoing redevelopment
3. A structure that is part of an industrial complex

Community Schools located in short-term detention facilities should assess the specific educational needs of the students detained there and formulate an individualized program for each. Meeting such needs of the students, and eliminating any disruption of their current educational process is the first step toward discouraging and preventing potential dropouts.

Community school programs can also be adapted for use as:

1. A room in a center for neglected and/or abused children
2. A detention camp or group residential placement home
3. Community day centers

Since Community Schools deal with youths who are deeply troubled, it is unwise to locate them near traditional high school campuses. Experience has shown that the proximity of young delinquents often leads to unrest and rebellious behavior on the part of the regular students.

Sites should be located near public transportation and adequate parking facilities. Generally speaking, school districts do not fund bus transportation for Community School students. Youths who attend Community Schools must find their own manner of transportation to and from the site.

FACTORS TO CONSIDER WHEN PURCHASING CURRICULUM MATERIALS

Before designing each curriculum and making purchases, it is important to take these steps:

1. Identify all areas of student need and the goals of the school.

2. Become familiar with the local site area and the state education code.

3. Evaluate previous student assessments and solicit input from previous teachers regarding the selection of instructional materials.

4. Find out which textbooks are favorably viewed by the traditional school's department heads. Consider purchasing softbound textbooks. (Students often prefer these to hardbound because they are smaller, lighter, and less overwhelming.)

Avoid the tendency to try to match the wide assortment of subject areas found in a traditional school. Keep in mind that the Community School deals with special youngsters who have special needs. Keep the curriculum consistent with those needs.

POSTPLACEMENT COUNSELING

It is advisable to have counseling services available for those students who are returning home after incarceration or detainment. These services can be used to review a youngster's academic achievement and to help develop goals for continuing her or his education. It can also assist the student to enroll in and adjust to a new school and to find community service programs that can provide additional support. (See Form 7–6.)

WHY COMMUNITY SCHOOLS ARE ESSENTIAL FOR DROPOUT PREVENTION

No community is free from crime or child abuse. The task of singling out incorrigible or abused youngsters and removing them from the school system for redirection or protection, as the case may be, is an unpleasant but necessary one for teachers and counselors. The Community School serves as a refuge or asylum for these young people and eliminates the problem created by having them dumped on the street. Educators faced with the need to get so-called "bad" or "troubled" youngsters off the traditional campus must be supplied with a place to send them. The Community School fills this need and supplies the initial remedial action that helps prevent dropout.

THE RESPONSIBILITY OF THE SCHOOLS TO REPORT SUSPECTED ABUSE

Every school is required by law to have a supervisor of child welfare available.

Teachers, nurses, counselors, principals, and other designated school personnel are often the first to notice the signs of child abuse and are mandated to report their suspicions. Physical injuries are the most obvious sign. But youngsters who chronically disrupt the classroom may be suffering from invisible physical injuries, from emotional injury, from poor nutrition, or even from depression. Sometimes counselors are forced to request protective agencies to investigate the home of a disruptive student in order to determine if the home is the cause of the child's poor behavior.

Most schools have developed special procedures for reporting suspected juvenile abuse. Reporting is an individual responsibility and each school employee should be made aware of the potential civil liability for *not* reporting. No one individual can depend on another to make known a suspected case. The law allows reports of suspicion of child abuse to be filed without fear of reprimand, retaliation, or penalty.

Agencies That Receive School Reports of Child Abuse

When maltreatment of a child is suspected, a report is made by school personnel and directed to a designated employee of an appropriate agency, such as:

1. The local police
2. The county welfare department
3. The Human Resources agency
4. The department of public social services
5. The county juvenile probation department
6. The county sheriff's department
7. The community safety agency

8. The awareness clinic
9. The action council

(The foregoing list is only a small sampling. Agency titles vary from city to city and from county to county.)

As a rule, the name of the person who reports suspected child abuse is kept confidential. However, it may be released as a result of certain court actions or court orders. Mandated reporters—that is, people, such as school personnel, who are obligated by law to report suspected child abuse—are required to give their names and addresses to the protective agency with whom they file. In the vast majority of cases, however, very few child abuse cases are so complicated that a court hearing becomes necessary. In these few instances, there is usually more than one reporter of the incidents of abuse that provoked the remedial action.

DO COMMUNITY SCHOOLS WORK?

Recently, a Community School in California computed the results obtained from records of their past year of operation.

It was found that 63 percent of the youngsters who attended that year *did not* become high school dropouts. Nearly one-third (28 percent) graduated or received their GED certificates, and one quarter (25 percent) returned to traditional campuses, while 10 percent continued their educations at other learning facilities in the county or district.

Of the remaining 37 percent who attended the Community School that year, 15 percent chose to stick it out at the Community School and continue to strive for a diploma. Their chief reason for staying was to remain with a compatible peer group. Since 90 percent of the youngsters attending Community School score two or more grade levels below their age group, many choose to remain at Community School in order to be with others who share the same skill problems. And they generate an increased confidence in their ability to catch up to their peers in traditional school by taking advantage of the individualized instruction they receive.

CASE HISTORY OF ROCKY: A HOSTILE TEENAGER

Rocky was thirteen when I first met him. He was streetwise, tough, crafty, and truant. He was one of six children sired by an alcoholic and abusive father. At the age of eight Rocky robbed his first store, which began a long history of minor arrests, community counseling, and a growing reputation for undisciplined behavior.

His last escapade had led to a required appearance before the School Attendance Review Board. There, based on the testimony of the police officer assigned to the narcotics division, the SARB removed Rocky from his school and required him to participate in the Community School sponsored by the county.

When Rocky walked into the office his hands were thrust deep into his pockets. His shoulders were slumped forward and his shuffled steps showed his reluctance to be where he was. It was plain to see that his attitude was one of complete indifference. He displayed so insipid a disposition that the hostility he was renowned for was perfectly concealed. He accepted the lesson assignments I gave him with a docile lassitude and responded to my instructions and directions with perfunctory, meaningless mutterings. When he left, I found my own feeling was one of apprehension. Despite my effort to instill within him even a small measure of motivation, I had the immediate sense that nothing I had said to him had penetrated his veneer.

When Parental Guidelines Are Missing

Rocky's record was full of petty crime and violence, and he was suspected of having contact with the underworld. He knew too much of the seamy side of life and not enough of the academic. His assessment test showed that his I.Q. was barely 90 and his skills were below grade level, yet his knowledge of crime was equal to that of someone in an entry-level position with the Mob.

When Rocky entered the Community School, his record showed he had been expelled for an entire semester for molesting a girl on campus. In addition, he had beaten a younger boy so severely that a charge of assault and battery had been levied against him. The consensus of staff opinion at the time was that the expulsion should have been permanent, or at least for a longer time. However, the state in which Rocky resided limited expulsion to one semester and mandated that the student be placed in some type of school program and given a chance to get an education.

The list of Rocky's misdemeanors included loitering around campus and possession of drugs. Although Rocky had never been caught selling drugs, it was common knowledge on the school campus that he dealt in the "heavy stuff." He had an uncanny ability to assess his customers, and even when he was approached by a narcotics officer in disguise, his sixth sense prompted him to make a gift of the joint to the narc rather than sell it to him.

Rocky was a prime example of a teenager who did not fit into the system.

How the Community School Helped Rocky

The court placed Rocky in a community day center, a group home where youngsters are sent when the court determines that their own homes represent an unstable environment and contribute to their delinquent behavior. Employing the technique of individualized instruction, Rocky's teacher worked with him toward long-term educational and behavioral goals. He was given drug and psychological counseling and aptitude tests and was placed in vocational training. During his twelve months in Community School, not only did Rocky's attitude improve considerably, but he gained the ability to read and write near his own grade level and acquired the skills to work as an auto mechanic, which gave him a new confidence in his own capabilities. Based on his excellent progress, he was placed in a foster home and began attending continuation high school. This young man was headed in the right direction at last.

The Community School was Rocky's salvation. It not only prevented him from dropping out but gave him a fresh start.

CASE HISTORY OF SAMUEL: A NEGLECTED CHILD

Sam was a rather good-looking boy of thirteen. He had straight black hair, olive skin, and soft brown eyes. He was average in height but slightly on the skinny side. Because of Sam's habitual truancy, he was referred to the home study program by the SARB. Sam was not into drugs or liquor, and he'd never been arrested for a criminal act. Sam's problem originated with his home environment. He was the offspring of illiterate parents who had no job skills—hence no money. Sam's parents were migrant workers who knew nothing except how to pick fruit and harvest cotton. The work was seasonal at best, and the wages were the lowest.

In his younger years, Sam's parental supervision was limited to the time his parents could spend with him when they were not working the crops. Because of their long absences, and perhaps also because Sam, after only a few years in school, had already gotten more of an education than his father, the relationship between the two was poor at best.

How Poor Environmental Conditions Play a Part

Sam lived in a shack in an undeveloped area of the city. When I drove up in front of Sam's residence, the first things I saw were empty beer cans and billy goats. A washing machine lay disassembled in the weeds that passed for a lawn and an offensive odor emanated from the dilapidated structure, lending a pungent emphasis to the impoverished condition of everything I saw.

Sam had missed a lot of school because of personal hygiene. The chances were that he had never been taught hygiene at home. But even if he had, there were still no facilities with which to bathe or shower or to wash clothes. There were times when Sam came to school smelling so bad that he disrupted the whole class and had to be sent out of the room. Most often, the school nurse was able to clean him up enough to return him to class. However, there were other times when he had to be sent home again. This was usually because he was infected with head lice.

Sam just never spent enough time in school to master the basic three Rs. As each year went by, he missed more and more school and fell further and further behind his classmates. The result was that Sam no longer understood what was going on in his own classroom, and he lost all interest, making matters worse.

How Decisive Action by the School Resulted in a Second Chance

In view of the circumstances of Sam's life and his academic history, the School Attendance Review Board decided that Sam would be better off if they reported his case to Child Protective Services.

This was a turning point in Sam's life. The agency took action. Working with the juvenile authorities, they removed Sam from his parents and relocated him in a foster home, improving his living conditions immeasureably. He was offered the opportunity to attend a Community School. With all this accomplished, Sam's case was no longer under the control or the jurisdiction of the local school district. Instead, county services took over and provided any further assistance Sam needed.

Today, Sam is striving toward a successful life in his new home and new school. He continues to communicate freely with his biological parents, but has no desire to return to his old life. His father and mother are more than grateful that their son has a chance for a better life and was able to avoid becoming a dropout statistic through the actions of the school district and their dropout prevention programs.

COUNTY COMMUNITY SCHOOLS

STUDENT REFERRAL AND INFORMATION FORM

Please type or print all information clearly. Return form to above address

Student's Last Name	First Name	Middle Name

Birth Date	Sex	Grade Level	Referral Date

District of Residence	School of Residence	Current Location of Student Records

Name of Parent or Guardian, Last, First, Middle	Home Phone Number

Street Address	Mother's Work Phone

City	State	Zip	Father's Work Phone

PROFICIENCY STATUS   PRIMARY LANGUAGE OF HOME   STUDENT'S ENGLISH ABILITY

Reading

Pass = 1

Math

No Pass = 2

Writing

1 = English
2 = Spanish
3 = Chinese
4 = Vietnamese
5 = Other
Specify_____

1 = Fluent
2 = Limited
3 = No English

ETHNIC GROUP

1 = Amer. Indian or Alaskan Native
2 = Asian or Pacific Islander
3 = Filipino
4 = Hispanic
5 = Black NOT of Hispanic origin
6 = White NOT of Hispanic origin

SPECIAL EDUCATION

1 = Yes
2 = No

PROBATIONARY STATUS

1 = 601
2 = 602
3 = Other
Specify_____

Probation Officer/Social Worker (if applicable)	Phone Number	Date of any scheduled probation action or review

What is your estimate of the student's problem regarding school?_____

What prior placements or interventions have been made in this student's behalf?_____

Signature of Person Making Referral	Phone Number

FOR COMMUNITY SCHOOLS USE ONLY:

Action Taken	Date	Teacher Assigned	Placement Location

Reviewed by

Form 7-1

COMMUNITY SCHOOL OPERATING PROCEDURES

BEHAVIOR:

1. Acceptable: Daily attendance, except for excused absences.
   A. Unacceptable: Cutting classes and actions requiring suspension.
   B. Consequences: Cuts and suspensions = no grade/credit. Excessive cuts or suspensions may lead to dismissal from program. Attendance is reviewed every 20 days.
2. Acceptable: Getting to class on time.
   A. Unacceptable: Being late to class.
   B. Consequences: Tardies effect your grade and credit. Excessive tardies may lead to dismissal from program.
3. Acceptable: Full voluntary participation in all school activities.
   A. Unacceptable: Refusal to participate in any school activity.
   B. Consequences: Conference with teacher. Possible suspension for remainder of day and/or next day. Continued nonparticipation shall result in dismissal from school.
4. Acceptable: Self-control; self-discipline.
   A. Unacceptable: Verbally or physically abusive behavior.
   B. Consequences: Conference with teacher. Possible suspension for remainder of day and/or next day. Dismissal from program.
5. Acceptable: Smoking in designated areas only, before school and during break. Keep in mind: *Smoking is a privilege and shall be restricted to designated areas only.*
   A. Unacceptable: Smoking in nondesignated areas during school hours.
   B. Consequences: Suspension for remainder of day and/or next day. Dismissal from program.
6. Radios and tape decks are not allowed at school.
7. Weapons are not allowed in school. Weapons that are brought to school will be confiscated. Bringing a weapon to school may result in dismissal from the program and possible police involvement.
8. Per State Education Code # _____ , using, selling, or sharing drugs or alcohol before, during, or after the program day, or suspicion of such use, is cause for early dismissal, suspension, or discharge, and/or police involvement. In our program, *suspicion of drug or alcohol use* shall result in suspension and/or police involvement. *Possession of drugs or alcohol* shall result in dismissal from the program *and* police involvement.
9. The school is closed to everyone except students who are currently enrolled and attending classes that day. Students are *not* to leave school *at any time* during the day without permission. Students *will* be suspended for the day if they are found in the parking lot or off campus during the school day.

NOTE: Items 1–5 are subject to modification dependent upon the circumstances and at the discretion of the staff.

Items 6–9 are state law and are not subject to the discretion of the staff.

I HAVE READ AND AGREE TO THE ABOVE OPERATING PROCEDURES AND I COMMIT MYSELF TO THEIR DAILY PRACTICE.

_____   _____
Student's Signature   Date

_____   _____
Parent/Guardian's Signature   Date

Form 7–2

TRANSCRIPT EVALUATION GUIDELINE

NAME _____ DATE _____ EVALUATOR _____ SCH. LAST ATTEND._____

STUDENT SIGNATURE _____ DATE _____ PARENT SIGNATURE _____ DATE _____

**** STUDENT CREDIT RECORD ****

CLASS OF_____ Subjects/Credits	Required	Credits Earned	Needs	Credits Earned	Needs	Credits Earned	Needs	Credits Earned	Needs	Com- pleted
English	30									
Math	20									
Science	20									
P.E.	20									
World History	10									
U.S. History	10									
American Gov't.	5									
Soc. Science Elective (PAG/Psyc/Law/Anthro)	5									
Driver's Ed.	2.5									
Health/Safety	2.5									
Consumer Ed.	5									
Fine Arts (Music/Art/Drama)	10									
IWE/OWE (30 max.)										
Electives: (70-85)										
TOTAL	210									

Form 7-3

STUDENT DROP LETTER

DATE: _____
TO: _____

    This is to inform you that _____
is being dropped from the Community School Program.

REASON FOR DROP

Failure to meet the following program requirements:

_____   completion of assigned hours of work per week.
_____   attendance at regularly scheduled meetings with
    instructor.
_____   other _____

_____

CURRICULUM

    You are responsible for returning the following curriculum materials immediately.

_____
_____

Instructor's Comments: _____
_____
_____

_____   _____
          Instructor   Administrator

BY STATE LAW, STUDENTS UNDER 18 YEARS OF AGE MUST BE ENROLLED IN SCHOOL.

Form 7–4

STUDENT PROGRESS REPORT

Juvenile Court Schools

Name:_____ Grade_____ Date_____ To_____

	Subject	Grade	Effort	Citizen-ship	Earned Hours	Comments	Teacher
1							
2							
3							
4							
5							
6							

Attendance days absent _____   Unexcused absences _____

	Effort	Citizenship	Attendance
A = Excellent			
B = Good			
C = Average	O = Outstanding	O = Outstanding	_____ Tardy
D = Poor	S = Satisfactory	S = Satisfactory	_____ Absence
F = Failing	U = Unsatisfactory	N = Needs improvement	
I = Incomplete		P = Poor	

cc: Office
     Student
     Teacher
     Probation Officer

Form 7-5

POST PLACEMENT COUNSELOR REFERRAL

	GRID NUMBER	LOG NUMBER

NAME OF PUPIL (LAST, FIRST, MIDDLE)	DATE OF BIRTH (MO/DAY/YEAR)	AGE	NAME OF SCHOOL

NAME OF PERSON WITH WHOM PUPIL RESIDES—TITLE OF PERSON AND RELATIONSHIP TO PUPIL	RESIDENCE TELEPHONE ( )

RESIDENCE ADDRESS—NUMBER, STREET (INCLUDE ANY NORTH, SOUTH, EAST OR WEST DESIGNATION), APARTMENT, CITY, ZIP CODE

NAME OF AFTERCARE AREA OFFICE, IF KNOWN	DATE PUPIL GOES HOME

REFERRAL CRITERIA	TEACHER RESPONSE		PS/TSA RESPONSE	
	YES	NO	YES	NO
1. Is the pupil between 14 and 17 years of age, with a career plan which supports his/her return to school?	☐	☐	☐	☐
2. Is the pupil 18 years of age, with a definite plan to continue his/her education such as vocational, adult or community college?	☐	☐	☐	☐
3. Is there a positive correlation between the age of the pupil and the number of credits earned?	☐	☐	☐	☐
4. Does the pupil appear to be a hard core gang member?	☐	☐	☐	☐
5. Does the pupil have a history of heavy drug and/or alcohol abuse?	☐	☐	☐	☐
6. Does the pupil show genuine interest in continuing his/her education?	☐	☐	☐	☐
7. Is the pupil designated as a special case, and therfore, deemed by staff to be appropriate for follow-up?	☐	☐	☐	☐
8. Does the pupil have an active I.E.P.?	☐	☐	☐	☐
9. Do you recommend counselor follow-up?	☐	☐	☐	☐
10. Check preference of pupil: ☐ Regular High School ☐ Junior High School ☐ Continuation School ☐ Community College ☐ C.D.C. ☐ Adult Education ☐ Occupational Center ☐ Does not wish to attend school				
11. Has transcript been sent to Division office?	☐	☐	☐	☐

COMMENTS OF TEACHER

SIGNATURE OF TEACHER	DATE SIGNED

COMMENTS OF PS/TSA

SIGNATURE OF PS/TSA (SPECIFY TITLE)	DATE SIGNED

COMMENTS OF ADMINISTRATOR FOLLOWING REVIEW

SIGNATURE OF ADMINISTRATOR	DATE SIGNED

FOR OFFICE USE ONLY

FORM COMPLETE	TRANSCRIPT RECEIVED	NAME OF COUNSELOR ASSIGNED/DATE ASSIGNED	SIGNATURE OF SECRETARY/DATE SIGNED
☐ YES ☐ NO	☐ YES ☐ NO		
☐ Case accepted ☐ Case declined	REASON		
☐ Case closed	DISPOSITION	SIGNATURE OF COUNSELOR	DATE SIGNED

Form 7–6

How Opportunity Programs Motivate Failing Students to Achieve

Some youngsters in elementary school do not acquire the basic skills needed to continue their education. Without basic reading, writing, and math skills, these pupils feel inadequate and find it difficult to keep up with the other students at their grade level. Should a student fail to learn the multiplication tables in the third grade, for instance, from that time forward math becomes a torture. It is impossible to learn division if one does not know how to multiply. By the time this pupil reaches junior high school, he or she is sadly unprepared for other subjects that involve math.

This holds true for reading and writing as well. The deficiency compounds as the student advances toward more complex studies. Unable to understand exactly what is transpiring in the classroom, the student merely "puts in time," which soon becomes boring. When it becomes so boring that he or she can no longer stand it, the student drops out.

DEFINITION OF A LEARNING OPPORTUNITY PROGRAM

A learning opportunity program is designed to help students who are academically behind other students their own age. Instruction is given in math, remedial reading, further vocabulary development, writing, study habits, and other survival skills. The teacher-student ratio is kept at no more than 1 to 10. This permits the teacher to individualize instruction in order to meet the separate needs of each student.

The public school systems that have implemented this program have adopted the following goals:

1. To help students attain a level of learning that is consistent with their chronological age

2. To enhance students' self-image by improving their basic skills

3. To gradually reestablish students in a regular classroom among peers of their own age group

4. To help students resolve their problems and eliminate their truancy

(Programs of this nature may be known by many different names. In this text they will be called Learning Opportunity Programs.)

THE EDUCATION CODE: A GUIDELINE FOR IMPLEMENTING OPPORTUNITY PROGRAMS

As always when you are considering a dropout prevention program, check your state's legislation to see whether funds are allocated for this type of program.

As a general rule, the education code will set the parameters for the program. It will authorize school districts to set apart a public school building, or a room or rooms within a public school building, for pupils in specific grades, to be known as opportunity school. The education code will also authorize a governing board to make rules and regulations for the program and to formulate an official statement of policies and procedures. It will set guidelines for participants by allowing for the enrollment of students who are habitually truant in elementary school, who score below average on standardized tests, and who have a history of discipline problems in the classroom. Some candidates will qualify in all three areas; others in one or two.

POLICIES AND PROCEDURES

The Learning Opportunity Program is one of the easiest dropout prevention programs to implement. Because the program is usually located on an established campus, many of the policies remain the same as those for any other classroom, and only the structure varies. Generally, the policy and procedures for an opportunity program will include the following:

1. An attendance policy that states the minimum school day (this is important for attendance accounting and apportionment funding)

2. Enrollment procedures and eligibility criteria

3. A description of testing methods and other evaluation procedures

4. A behavior code, including classroom rules and discipline procedures

5. Standards of proficiency and the general curriculum needed for graduation

6. The scope of instruction, with individually planned learning programs based upon educational assessments of each pupil

7. The grading policy (Pass/Fail or letter grades)

In formulating policies and procedures, it is very important to make a statement about the number of hours students are expected to attend school. Some programs are based on a four-period day, others on a six- or seven-period day. The important thing is to make a commitment and stick to it.

For a Learning Opportunity Program to succeed, it is vital that students stay in a core class with the same teacher for four periods each day. Additional class periods can be spent in physical education or in elective classes chosen by the student.

Giving pupils a chance to leave their core class creates in them a feeling of belonging to the regular campus and serves to enhance their self-image. At the same time, it begins the process of mainstreaming them back into the traditional system.

FUNDING

Youngsters in a Learning Opportunity Program generally attend school for the same number of hours per day as regular junior high students. Therefore, the funding for such a program should be based on average daily attendance and appropriated in the same way as for regular junior high programs.

It is wise to be sure that the program provides the option of offering a short day to junior high students. These students are at risk for dropping out. Profile information compiled by the Los Angeles U.S.D. Dropout Prevention/ Recovery Committee, 1985, indicates that characteristically they have a short attention span, irregular school attendance, frequent tardies, and are encouraged by their families to leave school. Existing Learning Opportunity Programs have successfully improved the attendance of at-risk junior high students by offering a shortened school day. For these youngsters, the apportioned attendance funds would be calculated according to the state's legally mandated minimum day. The education code that authorizes the program sets the guideline for length of day.

WHY OPPORTUNITY PROGRAMS WORK

In all recent studies, dropouts are characterized as poor learners with inadequate skills in reading and mathematics. (A large majority of dropouts begin remediation in the elementary grades.) They generally have low self-esteem, minimal self-expectations, and little regard for social values.

While there are no guarantees, a well-implemented Learning Opportunity Program has the potential to correct problems such as these:

Problem: Inadequate skills in reading and mathematics.

Solution: Individualized instruction with a teacher-student ratio of 1 to 10.

Problem: Student has low self-esteem.

Solution: Young people like to feel that they belong. Schools that generate a strong sense of affiliation are usually small. Teachers and students know everyone. The sense of "belonging" that the small opportunity classroom generates promotes self-esteem.

Problem: Poor social values and social immaturity.

Solution: As part of the curriculum, this program incorporates the teaching of social behavior and general counseling on matters relating to teenage social problems.

Students are motivated to learn when the material presented is on their grade level.

In the Learning Opportunity Program, students *do not* fail. Why? Because they are working at a level they can understand, and success in all subject areas becomes inevitable.

This type of academic success reinforces the students' self-image and tends to enhance their sense of belonging to a school family.

High-risk youths, which these students are, demand creative instructional methods that produce an atmosphere conducive to successful learning. Teachers can vary from traditional small group teaching methods and the curriculum can be designed to meet the needs of the individual student as well as the general school requirements.

WHY A DROPOUT PREVENTION PROGRAM IS ESSENTIAL FOR JUNIOR HIGH YOUTHS

The early teenage years are a period of sexual maturation, a time when numerous changes are happening within the adolescent body. Young girls undergo an increase in female sex hormones that eventually leads to the onset of menstruation. The emotional effects of monthly periods may cause alterations in the teenager's personality. Many of these, such as irritability, depression, or the inability to adjust to the new status of womanhood, are negative.

Teenage boys must learn to deal with changes just as dramatic. They have to adjust to such things as untimely penile erections, nocturnal emissions, and uncontrollable changes in voice pitch. These may lead to embarrassing moments in the classroom, or happen during innocent social interaction with girls. It is understandable that boys, faced with these body alterations, may be distracted from the teacher's lecture.

For these reasons, the transition from elementary school to junior high is an anxiety-provoking time of life. The youngsters are going through environmental changes as well as bodily changes. In elementary school there was one classroom, one teacher, and one class group with which to socialize and interact; in junior high, there are class changes, three to five different teachers each day, and classes that vary in population.

Youngsters who are emotionally immature, or who are having problems at home, are especially vulnerable to dropping out of school at this stage of their education.

The Learning Opportunity Program fills a need for youngsters who are not ready to handle the abrupt change from elementary school to junior high. It provides a smooth transition into junior high, and the individualized, self-paced instruction gives youngsters confidence.

THE REFERRAL PROCESS

Youngsters who are doing poorly in elementary school because of truancy, emotional trauma, poor academic skills, or poor social skills are the best candidates for a Learning Opportunity Program. These youngsters are generally referred to the program by teachers and principals of the elementary schools they attend.

In making the referral, the following guidelines may be useful:

1. Fill out a referral form and submit it to the junior high counselors. (See Form 8–1.)

2. Notify both parent and student in writing of the intended assignment. (See Form 8–2.)

3. Use the telephone to set up a conference with the parent, elementary teacher, student, and any other individual who may provide relevant information about the student's school history. A counselor or social worker may also be helpful.

4. Assess the student's academic skills and set up an educational goal. (See Form 8–3.)

5. Provide the student with information about the Learning Opportunity Program, classroom rules, school rules, and anticipated length of stay in the program.

It is important to review the progress of the pupil twice a year to see if she or he is ready to return to the traditional system. Students should be counseled to look upon the opportunity program as just that, an opportunity. Once they have made sufficient progress academically and emotionally, a return to the traditional system is warranted.

THE CURRICULUM

Because youngsters in the program are academically behind their age group, they may need curriculum materials at the second- or third-grade level in the areas of reading, math and language. As each student is assessed and her or his grade level is determined, the personnel can decide what books are needed and make a record of them. The administrator of the program can then ask elementary schools in the district if there are a few extra copies of the needed books.

A second option in getting curriculum materials is to anticipate the needs of the opportunity program and order an additional set of reading, math, and language books during the spring or fall general district book order. Generally, books can be used longer in an opportunity classroom because they get less use, are seldom checked out, and the material is so basic that it is almost never outdated.

It is important to keep the curriculum guidelines simple. The primary educational objective is to bring the students up to their academic grade level. Making use of more advanced technological equipment, such as computers, may be an added advantage, provided the equipment promotes the students' basic skills. However, it is not advisable to attempt to teach anything as complicated as computer literacy, for instance, or any other highly advanced subject. These youngsters need to concentrate on the basics.

STAFFING

Traditionally, it has been thought that junior high youngsters are the most difficult age group to instruct. Girls and boys often feel uncomfortable with each other, most likely because of the physical changes they are experiencing. Some twelve- to fourteen-year-olds are still quite immature. Many continue to have short attention spans and require more physical activity than that which is usually available to junior high youngsters.

With this in mind, administrators of Learning Opportunity Programs must hire teachers with special qualities. Teachers who take on pupils eligible for the program must be resilient and expect a challenge. These young people are difficult to teach. Staff members must be willing to sacrifice rigid schedules and adjust goal expectations in academic areas in order to meet the needs of their students.

It is recommended that program teachers hold credentials in both the elementary and the secondary levels. They must be able to teach reading and social skills and to supervise peer counseling. They must also be able to teach good study habits and enforce classroom rules while helping students to solve the personal problems that may be the source of their poor academic history. Good teaching skills, plus a background in handling troubled youths, are essential for opportunity instructors.

CASE HISTORY OF BOB: A BOY FROM THE STREETS

Short, chubby Bob had a chip on his shoulder, a poor self-image, and a defiant attitude. He was of average intelligence, but academically he was below average, mostly because of truancy from school. Peer ridicule and pressure from his "street family" caused him to skip school to roam the neighborhood.

Bob's father was an alleged member of the Mexican underworld. He handled drugs for the syndicate and was well paid for his efforts. He lived at home only when the "heat was on."

He was a poor role model for Bob. This was evident from the file reports at the elementary school Bob attended. Bob never got along well with his peers. There were incidents of stealing from desks, talking back to teachers, and striking other children during recess, plus a lot of absenteeism.

By the time Bob reached his preteen years, he had already been in juvenile hall twice, and the school district had used almost every available means to help him straighten out. The last attempt was a Learning Opportunity class, where he was required to attend only four hours a day and could learn at his own pace.

At first, this seemed to be the solution. With only ten other students in the classroom, Bob received enough personal attention from the teacher to fulfill his needs. He began to attend school regularly and his basic education skill doubled in only a few months. However, Bob was still experiencing peer problems at school, and his natural environment seemed to be the streets. Eventually his attendance waned and he dropped out of school.

The School Attendance Review Board reviewed his case and decided there was nothing they could do but remand him to the juvenile authorities. Bob went to juvenile hall for the third time.

While in juvenile hall, Bob expressed a sincere desire to turn over a new leaf. Although eligible for ninth grade when he was released from detention, he was far behind his peers academically. The school personnel extended themselves in an effort to do what they could to help. Reanalyzing his situation, the counselor made the decision to place him back in the Learning Opportunity Program on probation.

As part of Bob's trial period he was required to

1. Meet with a probation officer twice a week
2. See a school counselor once a week
3. Attend school on a regular basis

By the end of the year he was learning well enough to return to the traditional classroom with his peers.

The Learning Opportunity Program provided Bob with an environment and learning mode appropriate for his needs. It enabled him to catch up—something he might never have accomplished on his own. Although his home life could not be changed by the school, the one change that could be made was thoughtfully contrived and successfully executed.

REFERRAL TO OPPORTUNITY PROGRAM

Name _____ Age _____ Birth Date _____

Address _____ Home Phone _____

Sex:[M] [F] Current School _____

Counselor _____ Grade _____

Parent or Guardian _____

Address _____ Phone _____

Date of Referral _____

Reasons for Referral:

[ ]   Truancy   [ ] Poor social skills   [ ] Low self-esteem
[ ]   Low standard test scores   [ ] Poor classroom behavior
[ ]   Below grade level in math   [ ] Below grade level in language
[ ]   Other _____

Previous Action Taken:
[ ]   Detention   [ ] Parent conference   [ ] Modified day
[ ]   Interschool transfer   [ ] Psychological evaluation

Documents Attached:
[ ]   Proficiency records   [ ] Basic skills results
[ ]   Complete attendance records from grade one to the present

Consent to Referral

Signatures

Principal _____

Counselor _____

Parent or Guardian of Student _____

Other _____

Form 8–1

PARENT NOTIFICATION OF REFERRAL

Date _____

Dear Parent or Guardian of _____

(student's name)

_____ has been referred to the counselor at

_____ Junior High School for possible placement in the opportunity program

for the school year _____ to _____. This recommendation is neces-

sary because an overall assessment of your child's academic and social progress in

school shows that he/she may be in need of special educational services.

The junior high counselor will provide you with further information

about the program at the parent conference that has been scheduled for

_____ (date of appointment) _____.

If you have any questions please contact _____

_____ at _____ (phone number) _____.

Signed: _____

cc: Student attendance file

Teacher/Counselor

Form 8–2

STUDENT ASSESSMENT

Name _____ Grade _____

Birth Date _____ Program _____

Testing Data

_____

Date	Test	Results

_____

_____

_____

_____

_____

Communication skills
Illinois Test of Psycholinguistic Abilities
Peabody Picture Vocabulary
Writing Sample
Bilingual Syntax

Visual-Motor-Perceptual
Valett Test of Psycho-Educational Development
Slosson Drawing
VMI
Rutgers

Academic Achievement
Peabody Individual
Woodcock
Slosson Oral Reading Test
Keymath Spache
Gilmore
SAT

Emotional Development
Piers-Harris
Tennessee-Assessment Self Concepts
Sentence Completion
Vineland (social)

Names of people who gave tests: _____

_____

_____

Chapter 9

Organizing a Dropout Prevention Program That Motivates Pregnant Minors to Stay in School

In an age when highly educated, well-respected single professional women conceive babies via sperm banks or are serving as surrogate mothers, it is difficult for parents to teach chastity and celibacy to adolescents.

Just as the technological revolution changed the way people live, the sexual revolution changed people's attitudes toward promiscuity. There has been a steady erosion of the stigma attached to out-of-wedlock babies and premarital sex.

In these times, teenagers have illegitimate babies just to prove that they are mature and capable of handling their own decisions. Having a baby may even allow teenagers to attain an elevated status in their peer group. It is not unusual to discover that one young girl will want to become pregnant for the simple reason that one of her friends has a baby. The child becomes a treasure that belongs to the teenage mother—one that cannot be taken away like the keys to the family car.

In a pleasure-oriented and permissive society, sex has become a national obsession. It is seen in the movies, shown on television, discussed on every talk show, reported on by the news media, and given enormous attention in general. Bookstores that were once the haunts of scholars and families looking for knowledge and entertainment are now filled with romance novels, nonfiction books, and how-to books, a large portion of which revolve around sex. Withholding knowledge about sex from children until they are deemed "ready," has become impossible.

ILLEGITIMATE BIRTHS ARE INCREASING

Federal studies show that illegitimate births increased rapidly during the 1970s and 1980s. By 1985, approximately 20 percent of the babies born to teenagers in the United States were born out of wedlock. Almost one-third of the babies born to white teenagers, and closer to one-half of those born to teenagers of other races, were illegitimate.

Although most school districts throughout the nation have a compulsory full-time education requirement that must be met by all school-age children, it is surprising how little of this time is devoted to sex education. Many teenagers are misinformed or have delusions about birth control, conception, and the menstrual cycle. Fewer than 25 percent seek advice about contraceptives before their first sexual experience. Lack of accurate information almost always leads to unwanted pregnancies.

THE BURDEN TEENAGE PREGNANCY PUTS ON SOCIETY

There are two major consequences of teenage pregnancy. First, the teenager's education is usually curtailed. The pregnant juvenile is generally forced to discontinue her education entirely or interrupt it for an extended period of time. Society loses the economic contributions these young people would normally make if they were fully educated and gainfully employed.

Second, teenage mothers who are not high school graduates and must remain at home to care for a child usually join the ranks of welfare recipients, in many cases receiving aid from the federal program Aid to Families with Dependent Children. The public may find that it is not only paying for the birth of the baby through Medicaid, but that it is bound to support the mother and child for the next eighteen years.

SCHOOL SYSTEMS CAN HELP KEEP PREGNANT GIRLS IN SCHOOL

Although most states allow pregnant girls to attend traditional school throughout their pregnancy, many expectant mothers do not, for their own protection and that of the unborn child. Complications of pregnancy, including morning sickness, toxemia, anemia, and bladder infections, keep many youngsters at home even though they are willing to stay in school. Emotional stress and embarrassment are other factors that lend themselves to young expectant mothers' truancy.

School districts that provide a special program for expectant minors are highly successful in preventing dropouts. This type of program is an attractive alternative that allows the pregnant girl to continue her education and prepare for childbirth and parenthood at the same time.

THE PREGNANT MINORS PROGRAM

Generally located in a facility separate from the comprehensive campus, the program offers a curriculum consistent with the district's requirements, but with heavy emphasis on pregnancy and child care classes. These classes provide biological and sexual information not allowed in traditional classrooms. The young mothers-to-be find new friends in these classes and meet with persons who will give them the help they need to see them through the trying months ahead. The purpose of the program is manifold:

1. To provide a safe place for an unwed mother to attend school
2. To teach the seriousness of the situation while concentrating on prenatal care
3. To prepare the unwed mother for birth, infant care, and parenthood
4. To keep the pregnant minor in school
5. To provide an academic program that affords equal educational opportunity

IMPLEMENTING A PREGNANT MINORS PROGRAM

When establishing a new program or expanding an existing program, it is best to start with a written proposal to the governing school board. This proposal should incorporate such items as:

1. Definition, rationale, and program goals
2. Definition of student needs
3. Procedure for implementation
4. Facility changes and/or housing needs
5. Budget and staff needs
6. Definition of curriculum

See Chapter 6, Form 6–1.

Once a school district has the approval of the governing board, a planning or advisory committee is selected to launch the program. This committee usually consists of one principal, one teacher, one student, and one representative from a private or public agency.

SUGGESTED MEANS FOR FUNDING THE PROGRAM

Many states have legislation that provides funding for classes for pregnant minors. The superintendent of public instruction makes the computations that determine the extent of the state aid to be allocated for the program. If legislation does not already exist in your state, and no other funding is available, refer to Chapter 13 for steps to take to initiate legislation.

Distribution of the funds depend upon the location of the program. If it is located on the same site as a comprehensive school, the money is usually distributed by the principal of that campus within the limits of the local school budget. Separate programs usually have the distinction of being considered "special schools" and should be able to receive funds in the same manner as any other small school in the district.

Districts seeking start-up funds may want to pursue a grant from the federal government or other public or private sources. It may be possible to bid for surplus funds at the end of the school year. Look into the possibility that your state rewards districts that establish dropout prevention programs. Research creative ways to utilize existing laws that provide funds for various district purposes.

FINDING A WORKABLE LOCATION FOR THE PREGNANT MINORS PROGRAM

The safety of the young mothers and their unborn children is a strong factor in considering a location for the program that will house them. Generally, it is best to locate the pregnant minors program in a facility away from the busy traditional campus. However, it is not an absolute necessity. There are existing programs functioning perfectly well on regular high school campuses. Although the pregnant youths remain in a core classroom for most of the day, they do mingle with the other students and share the cafeteria, and they may use the gym for adaptive physical education.

Other factors to consider when choosing a site for the program include

1. The availability of funding
2. The availability of school property that is presently sitting idle
3. The ability of the school district to provide transportation to the site
4. Staffing requirements, which include a nurse as well as teachers and clerical help
5. Access to facilities that are frequently needed by pregnant women,

such as a place to lie down and a kitchen for warming much-needed snacks

Although you may feel thwarted if you cannot obtain funding for a new facility, there are many alternative options open to the resourceful investigator.

1. Look for vacant community buildings or residences whose owners are in search of good tenants.
2. Seek out portable buildings that are easily moved, remodeled, or expanded.
3. Consider an addition to the home economics wing of a high school in your district.

SUGGESTED CURRICULUM GUIDELINES

Credits earned by students in the pregnant minors program should be applied toward fulfillment of graduation requirements. The curriculum must parallel the traditional high school's curriculum as much as possible to eliminate interruption of the youngsters' progress toward their diplomas. It may be difficult to teach all the classes that individuals need, and curriculum demands may exceed the staff's qualifications. For instance, a home economics teacher hired to teach child care classes in the program may be unable to cope with advanced algebra or physics. There is no one solution to this problem. However, the following are some viable options:

1. Use independent study so the student may complete assignments at home. The students must spend time meeting with the regular class instructor each day, if only for a few minutes.
2. Counsel students to enroll in basic classes during their pregnancies and plan curricula that will help them complete the other courses needed for a diploma after their return to comprehensive school.

Instructors interviewed by the author agree that *the most important part of the curriculum in a young pregnant minors program is education in prenatal care, with an emphasis on nutrition, exercise, and safety.*

The child development curriculum should cover conception, growth of the fetus, normal and cesarean delivery, costs, termination of pregnancy, growth and development of the baby in the first year, care of the infant and young child, first aid, and an explanation and discussion of child abuse. The young mothers should be provided with life-size dolls to practice skills learned in this class.

THE REFERRAL PROCESS

Most pregnant minors are referred to the program by the school nurse or a counselor. The basic requirement for entrance is a note from the doctor relating the stage of pregnancy and the general health of the expectant mother. The only other eligibility stipulation is that the student must not have graduated from high school. It is best to start a youngster in the program at the beginning of a semester; however, the stage of pregnancy is the most important factor in the timing of the entry.

The referral process includes a few simple steps:

1. A written notice to the parents or guardian of the pregnant minor describing the program and suggesting referral (see Form 9–1)

2. A meeting between counselor, student, and parent to discuss an educational goal and curriculum plan

3. Completion of the referral form (see Form 9–2)

Districts that are presently using this program find that their largest problem by far is that the number of pregnant minors usually exceeds the space available in the program. It is important that during the referral process the duration of enrollment is stated *in writing* to both student and parent. Should the pregnancy exceed the time limit, the school can then release the student from the program to make room for other pregnant youngsters.

It is wise for a planning committee to meet at the beginning of every semester to study incoming referrals and review the eligibility of students currently enrolled in the program.

MEETING STAFFING NEEDS

Youngsters who participate in the pregnant minors program generally are not troubled youths. They are at risk for dropping out of school simply because of their pregnancy and the complications that arise from it. It is not necessary for teachers to have special counseling skills. Instructors who function well in the traditional classroom are competent to teach in this program.

It is wise to employ female teachers who are credentialed in the areas of home economics, psychology, and child care and development, and who have some background in teaching basic English and math skills. These educators are not hard to find. Most colleges require undergraduates who major in a nonacademic subject, such as home economics, to minor in an academic subject.

It is necessary to schedule a nurse to visit the classroom daily for at least an hour. This professional can participate in teaching first aid, answer questions from the students, address most medical problems, and help the students recognize the beginning of labor.

Because this is a program and not a school, there are no clerical needs that would require additional personnel. All attendance accounting and reporting is done by the teachers in the traditional manner and sent to a home school. If the pregnant minor population is large enough to warrant a separate school, the normal district procedure for staffing such a school would be followed.

The teacher-student ratio should be kept lower than in the regular district classroom. A limit of twenty-five pupils per teacher is recommended. In a two-room facility, for instance, the suggested staffing would be two teachers, one nurse, and one aide.

HOW TO KNOW IF A PREGNANT MINOR PROGRAM WILL LOWER YOUR DROPOUT RATE

Before implementing this type of program for dropout prevention, it is important to measure the population that will be served. Obviously, in large cities, it can be assumed there will be a large number of pregnant teenagers.

In smaller, more rural communities, you may need to analyze the county and city census reports or the statistics on births of illegitimate babies at local hospitals. Taking the time to compile a comprehensive list of youths who have dropped out of school may also give an indication of the percentage of pregnant minors in the community.

There are districts that run very small pregnant minors programs, serving perhaps ten to fifteen youngsters a year. The staff members in these special schools get a great deal of satisfaction from the help they give to these young people.

According to a report by the National Association of State Boards of Education, 49 percent of families headed by a female dropout live in poverty. Females almost always face severe economic penalties for dropping out of school. The less schooling a mother has completed, the more likely it is that her offspring will leave school before graduation. By helping a young mother stay in school today, school districts may be helping her offspring graduate from school in the future.

CASE HISTORY OF RAMONA: THE IMPACT OF TEENAGE PREGNANCY

Ramona's parents had the customary beliefs and values of a strict Roman Catholic family. The code of conduct for every family member was clearly understood. Instructions from the church must be followed and all church doctrine strictly adhered to. Giving birth to a child out of wedlock was not only scandalous, it was forbidden.

When Ramona missed her menstrual period, she began to pray. She didn't see how she could be pregnant. The only time she had had sexual intercourse, in the back seat of her boyfriend's car, it had been quick and painful. She had never repeated the experience again.

Ramona tried to live a normal life for the next six months. She attended classes at her high school, dated, and participated in extracurricular activities. However, the day came when she could no longer evade her mother's questions concerning her unusual weight gain and her pregnancy was divulged. Until this time she had no prenatal care.

The family was devastated by the revelation. They had expected Ramona to go on to college, meet a nice man, and get married when the time was right. Now it appeared Ramona would become a high school dropout with a youngster to raise.

Using a Pregnant Minors Program to Give Help

Ramona and her mother looked relieved when the program was explained to them. By enrolling in the program, Ramona could continue in her present classes and would not lose a semester during the last trimester and birth of her child.

With the baby due in January, it seemed feasible for Ramona to return to regular high school at the semester break. She could return to her second semester classes with all her senior friends and be on target for her original graduation date.

Using the Flexibility of the Program to Overcome Unexpected Complications

Plans sometimes have a way of not working out according to expectations. Perhaps because of Ramona's youth and the long period without prenatal care, she developed complications in the last three weeks of her pregnancy. She became very sick, the baby arrived late, and she was unable to pass her finals.

For the next three weeks, Ramona stayed home, nursed her baby, and spent almost every waking hour on her schoolwork. Rather than fail her, the instructors in the pregnant minors program allowed Ramona to make up the work she missed. She took her finals late and passed them.

Meanwhile, the counselor at her regular high school made it possible for her to enroll in new semester classes and concentrate her study on a few subjects. Three weeks into the new semester, Ramona was released by her doctor and allowed to return to regular classes.

The Program Helped Ramona

While Ramona's life has taken a different course because of the baby, the alternative school program provided her with the opportunity to keep her life on track and graduate. Without the pregnant minors program, Ramona very likely would have followed the pattern of other teenagers caught in her circumstances. She would have dropped out completely, sat home in seclusion, and missed the opportunity to continue her education while awaiting the birth of her baby.

PARENT NOTIFICATION OF PROJECTED REFERRAL

Date _____

Dear Parent or Guardian,

___(Student's name)___ has asked to participate in our Pregnant Minors Program during the _____ semester of the current year.

This program was designed to meet the needs of pregnant minors who have entered the second trimester of their pregnancy. The program provides a curriculum consistent with that of the regular high school, but with special child care and pregnancy classes. The purpose of the program is to prepare the mother for parenthood while emphasizing good prenatal care.

A school counselor will provide you with further information about the program at the parent conference that has been scheduled for ___(date of appointment)___.

We will need your permission to enroll ___(student's name)___ in this program. If you have questions that need to be answered before the conference, please contact _____ at ___(phone number)___.

Signed _____

Form 9–1

STUDENT REFERRAL AND INFORMATION SHEET PREGNANT MINORS PROGRAM

Student's Name _____

_____ _____ _____
Birth Date   Grade Level   Referral Date

_____ _____ _____
District of Residence   School of Residence   Location of Records

_____ _____
Name of Parent or Guardian   Home Phone Number

_____
Address: Street   (Apt. #)   City   State   Zip

_____ _____
Mother's Work Phone   Father's Work Phone

Personal History and Pregnancy Information

_____ _____
Doctor's Name and Address   Phone

_____ _____
Present Month of Pregnancy   Baby's Due Date

Put an X in the boxes that apply to you.
I have: ( ) Severe morning sickness   ( ) Frequent headaches
         ( ) Heartburn   ( ) Constipation
         ( ) Backache   ( ) Severe fatigue
         ( ) Hemorrhoids   ( ) Leg cramps
My doctor is concerned about:
         ( ) The possibility of a miscarriage
         ( ) My severe vomiting after meals
         ( ) The possibility of anemia or low hemoglobin
         ( ) A bladder or kidney infection
         ( ) The possibility of toxemia
         ( ) RH incompatibility
         ( ) My recent exposure to German measles
         ( ) Complications caused by venereal disease

_____ _____
Student's Signature   Parent or Guardian's Signature

_____
Office Use only
( ) Doctor's Note attached   ( ) Sent for Student Records

Form 9–2

Chapter 10

Providing a Program That Keeps the Unwed Mother in School

The future appears bleak for the more than one million teenage girls who become pregnant each year in the United States. Fifty percent of all teenage mothers drop out of school. Once out of school, they stand almost no chance of achieving marital stability or of finding success in the job market. When a child has a child, both of them face a life of dependency and poverty. Trapped at home with a newborn baby, the teenage mother is often forced to turn to welfare for support while neglecting her education in order to care for her child.

Child support payments from the baby's teenage father are rarely forthcoming, and are usually unrealistic to expect for several reasons. Teenage fathers frequently refuse to acknowledge their offspring, not out of vindictiveness, but simply to avoid responsibility. It is a dilemma that leaves teenage mothers alone and helpless. Those young men who do admit responsibility for the child they fathered are usually unable or unwilling to provide support. It is unlikely that the young fathers have enough income to make such payments, even if they should be ordered to do so by the courts.

Further complicating the teenage mother's life may be her relationship with her own mother and/or father. Many parents of teenage mothers are only in their mid-thirties, and quite busy with their own lives. Often these grandparents have difficulty adjusting to their new role. They may feel threatened by the presence of an infant, or, on the other hand, they may become overly involved in the grandchild's upbringing and nag the mother continuously. The increased tension between parent and teenager may result in the latter moving out of the parental home, seeking support from government sources, and living in poverty, alone with her baby.

Some teenage mothers-to-be make the streets their home, living as prostitutes, shooting heroin, sleeping in gutters, and traveling from city to city. They get no medical attention and have little knowledge of birth control and disease prevention. Without the security of a permanent home, they spend much of their time spaced out on drugs and receive no prenatal care, no guidance, and no constructive advice. When the pregnancy shows, they must leave the sex-for-hire market and no longer have any source of income. Lonely, hungry, and destitute, these youngsters are lucky if they are found by the authorities and taken to a clinic or an adolescent health care center. Their babies are subsequently born into poverty.

THE PUBLIC SCHOOL SYSTEM AND THE TEENAGE MOTHER: PARENTING PROGRAMS MAKE A DIFFERENCE

There is a growing awareness that with so many teenage mothers, the schools must increase their service role as substitute parents by providing prenatal and birth information, along with counseling and some child care services. Keeping young teenage mothers in school is seen as a critical step in breaking the cycle of dependence on the welfare system. Some public school systems have already started a parenting program to meet the needs of these youngsters. This program is not viewed as a solution to the teenage pregnancy problem, but as a means toward providing more guidance and more extensive education while keeping youngsters from dropping out of school.

It is not uncommon for a teenage student to purposely get pregnant merely to escape from a bad home. With the money she receives from welfare, she is able to move out of her parent's home and set up housekeeping on her own, however humble that home may be. She seems to feel that the baby will provide relief from her emotional pain and make life more tranquil. This feeling is reinforced by the baby's natural willingness to love back, be cuddled, and accept the mother unconditionally.

At first, no thought is given to daily demands such as hunger, dirty diapers, illness, and crying. However, when teenage mothers realize how much time, energy, and patience the baby needs they speedily become disenchanted and may even inflict emotional or physical abuse on the infant. Living alone is difficult even for mature adults and the teenage mother soon longs for the companionship of her peers and relief from her parenting role.

The parenting program offers the teenager an opportunity to escape from her self-inflicted boredom, to see her friends, and to get a break from child care. The program provides a needed service to the child-mother while diminishing the possibility that an innocent baby will suffer some form of abuse.

THE PARENTING PROGRAM DEFINED

The parenting program allows teenage mothers to work toward their high school diplomas while learning techniques of child rearing. Every student has access to child care services in a well-organized nursery.

The classes cover math, hygiene, nutrition, English, child care, and family management. While the mothers attend these classes, their babies are cared for in the school's nursery. Students are allowed to progress at their own speed while they work toward individual educational goals based on the requirements for a diploma or equivalency certificate. The credentialed teachers who oversee the facility generally have specialized skills in teaching early childhood education and spend time supervising the care of the very young babies.

The daily program typically consists of four class periods with an hour lunch break. The enrollment is kept at a maximum of twenty-five students per instructor to allow for the individualized instruction that is needed and to limit the numbers of babies who utilize the nursery at any one time.

The program has the following goals:

1. To offer an individualized program that allows the student to complete the necessary credits for a diploma

2. To offer a curriculum of concentrated study so students can pass the General Education Development test

3. To offer a curriculum that concentrates on parental training and lessons in child development

4. To bring teenage mothers back into the school system

Many of the rules and regulations surrounding the teenage mother's classroom conduct are more stringent than those imposed on regular high school students. Students in the parenting program must telephone the school themselves to report an absence or an intention to be absent. If they do not, they risk being dropped to make space for more reliable students.

Junk food and cigarettes are strictly forbidden for health and safety reasons. Lunch is prepared and served by the students as a practical application of their home management studies. Students are required to plan the weekly menu for the lunches and make up the shopping list, staying within the allowed budget. No leeway is given for mistakes in the budget and, as in real adult life, no extra funds are provided if the money runs short before payday. It is the responsibility of the supervising instructor to keep the funds in balance. However, it should be noted that funds are available under the federal lunch program for mothers and children.

The students change subjects each hour but remain in the same classroom with the same instructor. As part of their education, they rotate shifts in the infant care center between class sessions, taking care of the babies of fellow students while being supervised by a credentialed teacher and/or a certified nurse. When not in the infant care center, teenage mothers are free to pursue their studies.

THE STATEMENT OF POLICY AND PROCEDURES

When developing a statement of policies and procedures to submit to the school board for approval, it is wise to include the following:

1. A statement describing the program
2. A statement of the actual number of days the students will be in attendance (use standard district guidelines for the number of comprehensive school days per year)
3. Curriculum guidelines showing the activities and experiences that will develop and reinforce needed skills
4. Enrollment procedures and eligibility criteria
5. Standards of proficiency and classes needed for graduation from the program
6. The grading policy and the method of evaluating progress
7. Method of funding (including fees and grants)

FUNDING FOR A PARENTING PROGRAM

School districts that operate programs for pregnant minors have had great success with parenting programs. Generally, when legislation pertaining to child development programs is passed, state funds authorized for programs for pregnant minors are also made available for child development centers and for school-age parenting and infant development programs. It is wise to check for legislation in your state that allocates funds for these types of programs.

For purposes of funding the pregnant minors program, the attendance report submitted to the superintendent of public instruction will show the average daily attendance of students enrolled in the program who are not *also* enrolled in some other program. The money is paid by the state to the district just as it would be for any other district program.

To supplement funding, some districts ask parents to pay a fee for the use of the nursery. Usually, this is not a requirement, and therefore monies received from fees are considered surplus and used for the purchase of equipment or furniture.

WHO IS ELIGIBLE FOR THE PARENTING PROGRAM?

Screening youngsters who apply for the program is often a difficult and heartbreaking experience. Friends refer friends. Community counselors frequently call to refer hardship cases who are truly in need of education and access to the child care facility. It is difficult to know exactly what guidelines to use when limiting enrollment.

The following are the general guidelines used by school districts with active parenting programs:

1. Students must previously have been enrolled in a local high school, but must not have graduated.
2. Students must be between thirteen and eighteen years old.
3. Students referred from the pregnant minors program have priority.
4. The teenage mother's baby must be younger than three years of age.
5. The teenage mother must be unskilled and unable to obtain gainful employment.
6. The student must be unable to qualify for adult education programs.

Despite the age limit, some allowance is made for special circumstances. For instance, a nineteen-year-old unwed mother who has been out of school for a year may still qualify if school administrators believe that she could obtain her diploma while enrolled in the program. Perhaps a young mother of nineteen or twenty who was previously in a district school could produce substantial reasons why adult school would not fit her academic requirements for a diploma. These are a few examples of the many arrangements that can be made to keep a program brimming with students.

THE REFERRAL PROCESS

Referrals from the pregnant minors program provide the majority of candidates for the parenting program. Other applicants are referred by counselors in special community programs, most frequently rehabilitation organizations. Usually, applicants for the program far outnumber the spaces available, and there is always a waiting list.

In the unusual circumstance that a program needs to recruit individuals, it is a good idea to develop a flyer that explains what the program is and which students are eligible to enroll. These flyers can be placed at strategic locations in the community.

Referrals to the program should be made in writing and submitted to the evaluation committee. (See Form 10–1.)

The committee's duties usually include the following:

1. Judging the eligibility of applicant
2. Analyzing her educational needs
3. Evaluating her academic skills and setting up an educational goal for her
4. Arranging counseling, if needed
5. Deciding on an enrollment date

If the applicant is not legally an adult and responsible for herself, parental permission is necessary before she enrolls. It is wise to notify both parent and student in writing about the intended assignment to the parenting program. (See Chapter 9, Form 9–1.)

Before the student begins classes in the program, it is recommended that a conference be arranged between the parent, the student, and the instructor. During the conference, review the rules and regulations for the program, reiterate the eligibility requirements, and state the estimated length of stay.

Be sure the student understands that the program is provided as a service to help young mothers finish their education and that abusing the rules may result in expulsion from the program.

HOUSING THE PARENTING PROGRAM

The parenting program facility is usually small, containing two or three rooms. One room is used as an infant care center, another as a classroom. The kitchen facilities, which are a must for a child care center, may be either in the classroom or in a separate room.

The program can be located on the campus of a traditional high school or at another location. Some programs are currently functioning in rented sites in shopping centers, others in county-owned housing, and still others in portable buildings placed in a suitable location.

The factors to consider when choosing a site are:

1. The availability of start-up funds
2. The ability of the school district to provide transportation to the site
3. The staffing requirements (generally, fewer staff members are needed if the program is located on a high school campus)
4. Access to vocational training facilities

THE CURRICULUM

The parenting program attempts to provide its students with an educational opportunity equal to that of a regular high school. The curriculum should be consistent with district policies and guidelines. All classes taken in this program should be applicable toward the fulfillment of requirements for a high school diploma. Remedial courses should be available and all instruction individualized to meet the needs of the students.

Textbooks and other curriculum materials can usually be ordered with the general district book order in the spring or fall. However, it takes a resourceful individual to investigate and choose the best method for ordering other items, such as

1. Baby needs, including diapers, bottles, nipples, blankets, toys, and clothing
2. Materials used to supplement a discussion of postnatal problems and needs
3. Kitchen supplies, such as dishes, flatware, and pots and pans

The purchase of these items is dependent upon regulations governing the allocation of resources that are shared with other district programs. It may be wise for a member of the planning committee to discuss the matter with the district superintendent.

The parenting program may also provide opportunities for the young mothers to develop job skills that will enable a smooth transition from school to work. Arrangements may be made for the students to attend vocational education classes at a nearby high school or trade school or to take part-time jobs. Some programs have extended their child care facilities to accommodate teenage mothers who work a few hours each day.

STAFFING THE PARENTING PROGRAM

Staffing needs vary, depending on the location of the program. If it is located on a traditional high school campus, only teachers and aides are needed. It is recommended that the ratio of teachers to pupils be kept at 1 to 25. Most programs have one teacher and one assistant.

Programs that are located in a separate facility but have a home school where attendance is reported and all clerical work is completed will have the same staffing requirements as a program on a school site.

Volunteers can be an important element. It has proven to be a good idea to recruit persons from the community who have a special interest in working with small babies. The senior citizens' office in your area may have a list of older women and men who are willing to help. These people are a tremendous asset on days when the babies are exceptionally fussy or the curriculum schedule is overloaded.

CASE HISTORY OF DONNA: A COOPERATIVE UNWED TEENAGE MOTHER

Donna was an attractive fifteen-year-old with normal intelligence and a pleasing personality. Her teenage problems quite likely grew from the lack of a loving home. Her parents had spent most of their adult lives working in menial, low-paying jobs in a struggle to keep a roof over the family. They showed little concern for Donna's problems and spent only a minimum of time with school authorities. To her credit, and despite her troubles with truancy and poor parental role models, Donna still tried to get an education, attending school spasmodically.

Before her sixteenth birthday, while seeking from a boyfriend the love and attention she did not get at home, Donna discovered that her life was complicated further by an unexpected pregnancy. She turned to her school counselor for help.

How Unforeseen Pitfalls Can Complicate Existing Problems

Donna went through the pregnant minors program with success and was well into the parenting program when her troubles began to compound. By the time her baby was five months old, he had developed a history of chronic colds and flu, often resulting in serious ear infections. As a result, the baby was ill-tempered and fussy much of the time.

For the protection of the other babies in the program and their mothers, Donna was requested to keep her baby at home when he was sick. The frequency with which the baby was ill during the next six months prevented Donna from attending her classes with any regularity. There was simply no one at her home with whom she could leave the infant. She fell far behind in her studies and the program director was forced to drop her to make room for a student on the waiting list. Donna became a dropout.

How Caring Personnel Brought Donna Back into the School System

During the next year, Donna stayed at home, supported by welfare. She made several attempts to find gainful employment, but the combination of her youth, her lack of education, and her child's chronic illness presented an insurmountable barrier. The school counselors, however, remained in contact with Donna and repeatedly encouraged her to return to school, pointing out that she would have more success in her job search if she had a good education.

Donna was disheartened by her inability to support herself and her baby. Her vision of the future was bleak indeed, especially when she realized that sooner or later she would be strictly on her own and without even the meager succor her parents offered. She became even more concerned about her son and what lay in store for him. With all this in mind, she renewed her resolution to try once more to attain the education that would help her and thus her son.

How Persistence and Determination Can Pay Off

A few months later, Donna was accepted back into the parenting program, and with her new-found determination and strength, she progressed very well. An evaluation of her transcript showed that it would take another three and a half years for Donna to graduate. She would be eligibile for the parenting program for only another six months. Realizing that she needed quick success, her counselor suggested that she concentrate on her basic academics and attempt to pass the General Education Development test (GED). A passing score on the test would entitle her to waive many credits needed for a diploma and shorten the time it would take her to finish school.

The GED certificate would also qualify Donna to enter a junior college or vocational school. Armed with upgraded skills or a trade, Donna would find it much easier to earn a good living, get off welfare assistance, and move to a better section of the city.

It is satisfying to report that through her own determination and persistence, Donna did succeed in passing the GED test. She then entered a local junior college and utilized its child care services while she pursued her studies further.

Thanks to the parenting program, caring counselors, and teamwork, Donna got the help she needed when the odds seemed against her. She is no longer just another high school dropout.

STUDENT REFERRAL AND INFORMATION SHEET
PARENTING PROGRAM

Student's Name _____

Birth Date	Grade Level	Referral Date

District of Residence	School of Residence

Name and Address of School Previously Attended

Location of Student Records (Name and Address of School)

Name of Parent Or Guardian	Home Phone Number

Address: Street   (Apt. #)   City   State   Zip

Personal History

Your Doctor's Name	Address	Phone

Your Child's Name	Birth Date	Age

Child's Doctor	Address	Phone

Signature of Student	Signature of Parent or Guardian

Office use only

```
( )  Child's immunization record    ( )  Parent permission slip
( )  Student file, including:       ( )  Other _____
     Attendance report
     Transcript and test scores
```

Form 10–1

Alternative Programs That Provide Adults with an Opportunity to Finish High School

In addition to the educational provisions made for youngsters under the age of eighteen, there are also programs that provide opportunities to bring adult high school dropouts back into the public school system where they can complete their education.

Returning to an educational establishment is as important to adults as it is to youngsters. School is not only an institution where academic skills are learned, but an environment that increases people's knowledge of the world while providing career opportunities and teaching the responsibilities of good citzenship. Adults can profit both economically and emotionally from their return to school.

Until the early 1960s, few programs were available to adults who had not earned a high school diploma. People who left school were stigmatized as dropouts and could seldom escape that label, even after learning a trade from a well-qualified craftsman.

To combat this situation, some states enacted legislation that provided for the development of several new kinds of schools and programs. These included community schools and alternative schools that gave adult students the freedom to decide what and how to study to complete their diploma requirements.

Three of these programs—the GED study course, independent study (adult education restart), and the external diploma program—will be discussed in this chapter. R.O.P., which also serves adults, was discussed in Chapter 6.

STEPS IN IMPLEMENTING ADULT DROPOUT RECOVERY PROGRAMS

Based on studies of the enormous, nationwide high school dropout problem, most states have enacted laws that allow for the set-up and funding of dropout retrieval programs for all age groups. It is generally the intent of the legislature to provide greater flexibility for schools and school districts so that they may better coordinate funding and program options to serve the needs of everyone in the district. The authority to initiate these programs is focused at the school level, with the principal and a program planning committee in charge.

The program planning committee should follow these steps:

1. Submit a plan to the superintendent of schools that describes the school's projected curriculum and the method that will be used to motivate students to complete requirements for a diploma.

2. Evaluate staffing needs, housing needs, and the proposed method of funding, and prepare a written statement about them.

3. Establish written policies and procedures for the program, including a definition of the population to be served, methods to attract prospective students, guidelines for enrollment, diploma requirements, and a drop procedure.

4. Make a presentation to the school board.

SOLVING ENROLLMENT PROBLEMS

Because adults volunteer to attend school and are not required by law to do so, it is more difficult to keep adult dropout prevention programs filled with students. The following have proven to be effective ways of finding and stimulating enrollment and participation.

1. Print information flyers about the program and distribute them in the community.

2. Advertise the program in the local newspaper, on television, and on radio.

3. Send letters explaining the program to county, city, and state agencies, including social security, welfare, and employment offices.

INDEPENDENT STUDY AS AN ADULT EDUCATION RESTART

Restart adult education, also known as continuing education, is instruction for adults seventeen years of age and older. It includes courses in a wide variety of subjects, correspondence classes, lectures, and organized learning activities. Until recently, outside activities, such as apprenticeships, were not included as part of the diploma program. However, some states have opened the doors, allowing adults to receive credit for independent study so long as it is under the weekly supervision of a credentialed teacher and structured by educational objectives and guidelines. These credits count as valid units toward a high school diploma.

For example, a housewife who has taught herself to sew can pursue the further development of her skill as part of a home economics class. A housewife who is adept at household bookkeeping can expand her skills away from the household budget to include more complicated office bookkeeping skills—all for high school credit.

The states that have laws providing for this program have designed it exactly the same way as the independent study programs for the kindergarten through twelfth grade (see Chapter 4). To validate such a program in your district, the district governing board needs to adopt written policies and procedures that define the nature and scope of the program, then follow the general procedure for implementation of a district dropout retrieval program. (See Chapter 4, pages. 53–56.)

Curriculum for Independent Study Programs

The courses should be designed to fit the individual educational needs of participants, including the need to fulfill diploma requirements.

However, adult education can differ in many ways from the education of younger students. Often, adults desire to learn a skill they can make use of immediately. They are more anxious to have recourse to vocational training classes or individualized independent study subjects. Adults have more experience than children, and their instruction plans should reflect this. In the search for a diploma, and using the independent study mode of instruction, the adult student can take the same classes that are required in traditional school for adolescents, plus more advanced classes.

Textbooks used in independent study are the same as those used in the local high schools of that community. Usually no fee is charged for classes or books because the state funds the program, just as it funds similar programs for youths. Money is paid based on hours of schoolwork reported and is calculated weekly.

THE GENERAL EDUCATION DEVELOPMENT TEST PROGRAMS

A major testing program that is recognized nationally has provided adults with a high school equivalency certificate since 1942. The General Education Development (GED) test is administered by departments of education in all fifty states. Adults who pass the test receive a certificate that is recognized by a great number of employers as the equivalent of a high school diploma. The certificate can also be used as credit toward a traditional high school diploma. In some states the certificate is recognized as a diploma.

Many states are implementing alternative programs with classes that are designed to help students prepare for the GED test. Major textbook companies have published study guidelines that may be utilized in these classes or in home study. Adults who have dropped out of high school may enroll in these programs and complete their education.

GED Test Programs May Vary According to the Guidelines Set Up by the School District

In some states the adult students attend classes until their instructors feel they are ready to pass the GED test. After the students pass the test, they are issued a certificate, along with a high school diploma from the district school. At that time, they become high school graduates, and no other classes are needed to fulfill diploma requirements.

Other states do not recognize the GED certificate as equal to a high school diploma, and no district diploma is issued after students pass the test. In these states, students desiring a diploma must take and pass other classes before they fulfill all the requirements needed to graduate. (See Form 11–1.)

Students who choose to have the GED credited toward a high school diploma would still need to complete American History, World History, American Government, Health/Driver Education, and Consumer Education and Economics to receive a district diploma.

There is no definitive method for setting up a diploma-oriented program based on the GED. The important thing is to follow the district procedures and guidelines that were implemented when the program was originally set up.

If the program is consistent and credible, the community and the district will give it the support it needs to become a successful dropout retrieval program for adults.

The GED: A General Outline

What is it? The GED consists of a series of five tests, in writing, social studies, science, reading, and mathematics. Each test is one to one-and-a-half hours long. The tests are available in Spanish, French, and English, and in Braille, large print, and audio tapes.

In 1988, based on a decision made by the American Council on Education, states will be required to add an essay question to the test.

Why take it? Adults who pass the GED may apply for a high school equivalency certificate by sending an application, the fee, and their official score to their state's department of education. In some states, the tests can be used to help meet the requirements for a high school diploma.

Who is eligible to take it? Applicants are accepted if they do not possess a diploma and if they are not presently enrolled in secondary school (though they may be enrolled in adult education classes). They must also be at least eighteen years old. An exception is made for seventeen-year-old local residents who are not enrolled in school but who would have graduated with a regular high school class, or who show a written request from a prospective employer or a military or postsecondary institution.

THE EXTERNAL DIPLOMA PROGRAM

The external diploma program is an alternative high school program for adults who have acquired skills through their life experiences. It is designed to appeal to the skilled laborer and is used as an alternative to the GED.

The philosophy behind the external diploma program is similar to that of some colleges and universities, which offer nontraditional external degree programs to people who demonstrate a high level of knowledge and expertise in a specific academic area. These institutions assign credits for work experiences, which may include books published or workshops attended, on the basis of sufficient documentation of these activities or accomplishments. The secondary-level external diploma program issues class credits for cultivated life skills, which can include household management, banking and money management, craftsmanship, and similar abilities.

Applicants are given as many as sixty-four competency tests that evaluate academic skills in various areas, including math, English, science, reading, and language usage. These tests help students identify their deficiencies in the basic skill areas. Students are then given an educational goal and sent to the community to utilize any educational resources that are available and will correct the learning deficiency. It is necessary for readers to research their own community for educational resources that may be utilized. Check for a computer literacy program, evening remedial adult education classes, businesses that offer night classes, and county programs such as English as a Second Language (ESL), enrichment classes, and volunteer literacy classes.

In the second phase of the program, students are once again given as many as sixty-four generalized competency tests. If all the deficiencies have been corrected, the student will receive a passing score and academic credit.

In a third phase of the program, students must demonstrate competency in one of three skill areas: occupational, special, or advanced academic. Students can demonstrate their skills through a variety of documentation forms, or by taking more advanced and complicated tests.

Why This Program Works as a Retrieval Program for Adult High School Dropouts

People who drop out of high school will sometimes continue their education if they are self-motivated. Choosing to drop out of the educational system does not mean that a person has stopped learning. However, people who are self-educated have no way to document their level of education. Because society demands some form of proof of educational achievement, dropouts must carry the stigma of failure unless the school system provides a means for these people to record their academic progress.

The external diploma program is the vehicle adults can use to acquire the documentation they need. Once their competency is substantiated, the diploma is issued and the student is no longer a high school dropout.

Surveys of external diploma program graduates show that they have an increased sense of self-esteem and an increased interest in continuing to learn, and that they receive job promotions and raises never before offered to them.

CASE HISTORY OF DIANE: A NEW BEGINNING

Twenty-year-old Diane had quit school in the second semester of her senior year to stay home with her mother, who was ill with terminal cancer. She was the oldest of six children, attractive, articulate, and scholarly. The rest of the adults in the family had ceased to be accessible to the children, leaving Diane with all the responsibility.

By the time her mother died, Diane had been out of school two years. She alone was responsible for her brothers' and sisters' welfare. She paid the bills, budgeting what little money the family received from Social Security and welfare. In addition, she solved disagreements between her siblings, kept the house clean, provided decent meals, and helped her brothers and sisters with homework. She was an industrious person, but going back to school was a luxury she could not afford during those two years.

Although she was saddened by her mother's death, Diane also experienced a sense of relief because it eased the burden for her. No longer a full-time nurse, Diane was able to organize the chores so that all the children participated in helping with the daily routine. Diane finally had time to finish her education.

Why the External Diploma Program Was a Good Choice for Diane

Before Diane was forced to quit school, she had been an excellent student. She needed only one more semester to graduate. Her basic competencies were reinforced continuously as she nurtured and taught her siblings.

She taught herself budgeting and bookkeeping skills, and during her mother's illness she learned nursing skills under the hospital's guidance. Although Diane was forced to drop out of school, she never stopped learning.

The external diploma program suited her needs. With this program there are no deadlines to meet, no tardies, and no unexcused absences. Although it is considered preferable for the student to spend twenty hours a week studying, exceptions are the rule. Instructors understand that adults in this type of program have unusual demands on their time. The hours are flexible.

Diane continued with the program for a full spring semester and into the summer. By fall, she had completed the necessary credits and was awarded her diploma. To show her gratitude to the school system, she attended a school board meeting. There she publicly thanked all those involved in her recovery. With her diploma in hand, she said to the school personnel, "If you hadn't enrolled me in this program, I wouldn't be standing here holding *this!* Thank you . . . all of you."

GED CHART

The following chart shows an example of the General Education Development test used in combination with other classes to earn the necessary credits for a diploma.

A.   District Diploma Requirements

English	– 30 units	Civics (American Government)	– 10 units
Science	– 10 units	Social Science	– 10 units
Math	– 20 units	Electives	– 90 units
U.S. History	– 10 units	World History	– 10 units
Consumer Education	– 10 units	Health/Driver Education	– 10 units

B.   The General Education Development test used to meet specified requirements.

English	–Up to 30 units if score on Test #1 is 50 or better.
Science	–Up to 10 units if score on Test #3 is 50 or better.
Math	–Up to 10 units if score on Test #5 is 50 or better.
Electives	–Up to 90 units if *average* test score for the five tests is 45 or more.

Form 11–1

How a Home Study Program Can Bring Home-Schooled Youngsters Back to the School System

More parents than ever are choosing to teach their school-age youngsters at home. The actual number of children meeting their compulsory education requirements in this manner has increased 500 percent since the early 1970s.

This new trend has produced a growing nationwide controversy between parents who wish to teach their offspring at home and the administrators of the public school system. The number of court cases concerning the parental right to educate youngsters at home has soared.

Until quite recently, most states did not recognize home instruction as a way of satisfying compulsory education laws. State education officials were prone to prosecute, and sometimes jail, those parents who literally forced their children to be "truant" when they kept them home and taught them themselves.

Because there is, at present, no firm definition of what actually constitutes a school, the courts in some states have ruled that a home can contain a school—just as part of a home can become an office for a self-employed business person.

On the other hand, some states still claim that compulsory school attendance laws require children to be educated either in public schools or in licensed private schools, restricting at-home instruction to a supplemental role. This judgment is based on the legal stipulation that a legitimate school must be staffed by certificated instructors.

Some parents who chose home instruction have found that it entails a bigger commitment than they had anticipated. Many later desire to enroll their offspring in public school, but are reluctant for fear of reprisals from school authorities.

Across the nation, a loose network of organizations has sprung up to help parents who choose home schooling in their conflicts with courts and public school officials.

Faced with definition problems, possible violation of First Amendment rights, and the lack of clear and precise guidelines for home instruction, the courts are still struggling for a solution to the conflict. Although every state now has laws that permit home instruction, the guidelines remain vague, the procedures sketchy, and enforcement efforts inconsistent. There is an overwhelming need for a consensus regarding home schooling.

Some states allow it only for kindergarten through grade eight, others only for youngsters who are homebound because of severe or crippling illness.

It is generally accepted that home schooling works well when the parents are well-educated and the students are precocious children who learn best in less formal, more individualized settings. However, administrators may wonder if home schooling is a wise choice for the average or below-average child who is having trouble adapting to regular school for any of a variety of reasons.

Despite these problems and concerns, the number of parents who are teaching their children at home continues to grow. Their reasons include the following:

1. Dissatisfaction with the public school curriculum and its use of textbooks that the parent considers unacceptable

2. Fear of violence, drug use, and excessive peer pressure to violate family morals

3. Lack of transportation to or living too great a distance from the closest district school

4. Religious beliefs or longstanding religious tradition

5. Disapproval of the teaching of sex education in the schools

6. Desire to spend extended time with their offspring

7. Concern over the appropriate use of corporal punishment

8. Concern over quality of education

NEEDED: A PROGRAM FOR PARENTS WHO WANT TO TEACH THEIR CHILDREN AT HOME

The problem of providing adequate and legal home schooling can be solved by the organization of a district-controlled study program. Educators worried about the quality of home education will be able to relax only when it is regulated by the public school system and textbooks and curriculum are approved by the district. Reasonable regulations and safeguards for the length and number of school days per year, consistent and adequate competency testing, and standards for promotion need to be established in every state.

State and local school officials have trouble accepting home instruction when the curriculum is heavily influenced by politics or religion with little or no attention to state education codes. Setting well-thought-out standards for home instruction would assure uneasy education officials that the children will not suffer from an inadequate curriculum or incompetent teaching. It would also lessen the danger of having home schools that concentrate on religious indoctrination to the exclusion of other studies.

Many administrators think that it makes good sense to build bridges between the school system and home-schooling parents, and envision great benefits from an organized home study program. States that have implemented programs along these lines have had great success in bringing home-instructed children under the auspices of the school system. Participating in such a program ensures a better rapport and understanding with parents while relieving them of the burden of coping with the technicalities and expense of qualifying their home as a private school when this is required by their state. In many cases, parents welcome the opportunity to make use of public school textbooks and other resources and are grateful for the guidance and direction available from school authorities.

Here are some of the benefits of a home study program:

1. The truancy rate is lowered by bringing home-schooled children back under the control of the system.

2. Lost federal and state funds are recaptured.

3. The home instructor is provided with professional supervision and materials.

4. Trained school personnel have the opportunity to identify cases of child neglect or abuse.

5. Competent school personnel can help set educational goals and organize curriculum guidelines.

6. The parent-instructor acquires a better understanding of attendance requirements and record-keeping.

DEFINITION OF A HOME STUDY PROGRAM

A home study program provides instructional assistance, curriculum materials, adequate testing materials and procedures, and other resources to parents who wish to instruct their children at home. As an alternative to classroom instruction, it makes every effort to remain consistent with the school district's established curricula and attendance procedures. The course of study is based on a written contract and is considered to be a full-time program that meets the educational needs of the student.

A typical program has a director who puts together a learning plan with the parents and students and then monitors progress through regularly scheduled visits by certified teachers. During the visits, the teacher records the student's attendance based on the hours of school time the student has logged, evaluates the knowledge gained by the student, and guides the student toward the successful completion of the predetermined educational goal. Schools are able to collect state funds for the program based on a record of the average daily attendance.

Home study programs can take a variety of forms in addition to this one. Some districts use a version of contract independent study (see Chapter 4); others base their programs on the community school model (see Chapter 8). Still others have created new kinds of individualized home study, such as the Centralized Correspondence Study program employed in Juneau, Alaska, in which credentialed teachers monitor students' work by mail.

DEFINITION OF THE HOME AND HOSPITAL STUDY PROGRAM

Most school districts in the nation provide tutoring for students who are unable to attend school because of serious illness or injury. A fully qualified and credentialed teacher is assigned to visit the pupil's home for the duration of the indisposition and supply the same instruction and guidance as the child would receive in school.

The usual policy of the home teacher is to confer with each of the student's on-campus instructors and follow the patterns already established in each class. Particular attention is paid to maintaining consistency in homework assignments and periodic testing. This practice assures that tutored students have every opportunity to preserve their academic standing and not fall behind their classmates.

Without this program, youngsters who miss classes for an extended period might become at risk for dropping out. The program gives them the peace of mind and concentration needed for speedy recovery. The fact that tutored students receive one-on-one teaching sometimes results in their learning more than they did in the regular classroom, which helps them make up for the study time lost during medical treatment.

The home and hospital study program is a viable and essential part of every school program. However, it is separate from the home study program and is not designed to bring truant youths back into the school system. These two types of programs should not be confused with each other.

HOW TO IMPLEMENT THE HOME STUDY PROGRAM

First, the local school board should adopt written policies and procedures for the program's operation, including a statement of the state education code relating to home instruction.

The manner in which programs are organized is strictly up to the school district. In every case, the most important elements are clear procedure guidelines. The more precise the program's definition of purpose, the better it can maintain its credibility. These guidelines should include:

1. An attendance policy that states the minimum number of hours per day that must be spent on schoolwork

2. Procedures for keeping attendance records (these must be in line with state attendance policies)

3. Enrollment procedures and eligibility criteria

4. A description of the plan for student evaluation, including standardized testing that meets district requirements

5. A statement of the scope of instruction, with individually planned learning programs based upon an educational assessment of each pupil

6. The grading policy and curriculum needs

THE RECRUITMENT COMMITTEE: AN IMPORTANT PART OF THE HOME STUDY PROGRAM

One of the most important aspects of a successful home study program is a recruitment committee, whose chief function is to educate the public about the program and identify the students who are learning at home. Parents who have been frightened by school authorities are often reluctant to pursue any program affiliated with the public school system. It is vital to the program to publicize the fact that any student not currently enrolled in a public school can apply directly to the home study program without fear of legal reprisal.

The following have proven to be effective ways of finding homeschoolers and stimulating their enrollment:

1. Print informational flyers about the program and distribute them throughout the county.

2. Advertise the program in the newspaper.

3. Notify the county and district public and private school principals about the program and supply them with flyers.

4. Send letters explaining the program to county and city agencies, including social security, welfare, and state employment offices.

ENROLLMENT PROCEDURES

The first step in enrolling a family in the home study program is to arrange a conference between the director and the family. The director starts by interviewing the parents. If the director is satisfied that the parents are sufficiently committed and competent to educate their children at home, the enrollment procedure progresses. The family is asked to complete an enrollment form (see Form 12–1) that will be delivered to the recruitment committee for approval, which depends on the guidelines set by the admission board for the program.

If, however, the director feels that the parents are unable to successfully instruct their children, other options are offered to the parents. Usually the director has a list of other alternative programs, private schools, and community services. Generally parents find an option that suits their needs. In the unlikely event that parents decline to pursue other options, their files are stored. After an acceptable period of time, the director may choose to offer the family a second chance to enroll in the program. No legal measures are taken.

The second step in the enrollment procedure is to assess the pupils. While they are being tested, the parents are asked to complete a registration package that includes immunization records, a request for records from previous schools, and other information that may be pertinent to the youngsters' education. (See Form 12–2.)

The third step is to draw up a contract. Once the test results are evaluated, an educational plan can be designed for the student. This plan will include the range of subjects a student will take, acceptable educational objectives, and the curriculum suggested for achieving them.

The contract (Form 12–3) is the basic document for audit functions and attendance accounting. This agreement should cover:

1. The system of student work evaluation

2. A statement of major objectives to be reached by the student

3. A schedule for completion of these objectives

4. The materials to be used by the student to achieve the objectives

5. The time and frequency of visits with a professional supervisor

6. Methods of obtaining assistance or tutoring

SPECIFIC PURPOSES OF THE WEEKLY MEETING

An important part of the home study program is the regularly scheduled meeting between school personnel and the homeschooling family. Usually, these meetings are held once a week. The purpose of the meeting is to

1. Verify that the students have fulfilled the minimum requirements for study time by checking their time log (see Form 12–4)
2. Test the students to determine what they have learned since the last meeting
3. Provide supervision, incentive, and instruction.
4. Issue new work assignments and collect past assignments (see Form 12–5)
5. Resolve current problems

If the guidelines for the district's home study program do not call for a weekly meeting, other methods may be used to verify attendance and evaluate student progress. These methods must be stated in the guidelines for the program and be approved by the school board and/or state department of education.

STAFFING THE HOME STUDY PROGRAM

Generally, this program caters to students from kindergarten through eighth grade. It is, therefore, preferable to engage teachers who have had a few years' experience in the elementary classroom. Experienced teachers generally have a collection of lesson plans and a knowledge of the district curriculum and materials. Teachers who are new to the district do not have these resources; in addition to developing lessons for each student and acquainting themselves with general district policy, textbooks, testing procedures, and curriculum guidelines, they have the added burden of learning the policies and procedures for an alternative program. This would be an overwhelming task for most first-year teachers.

Staff members must also feel at ease when negotiating with parents concerning the educational needs of their offspring. Teachers who prefer to leave meetings with parents in the hands of counselors or other administrators are not good candidates for the home study program.

FINDING SUITABLE HOUSING

It is not necessary to seek funding for a new room or building to house a home study program. The program can function well in existing classrooms located on traditional school campuses, in portable housing, or in a room within the county office of education.

The following is a list of helpful hints for finding a workable location:

1. Look for school property that is sitting idle.
2. Seek access to a quiet room where enrolling students can be tested without interruption.
3. Investigate the availability of a storeroom or shelving for books and supplies.
4. Be careful to select a room that can be used for parent conferences and counseling, as well as for the director's office.

Some programs function well in one room, with the director's office in the corner. Here, testing and conferencing are scheduled in the morning, and instruction in the afternoon. Other programs opt for two- or three-room facilities so one room can be used for storage, another for testing and conferences, and a third as a classroom.

It is wise to take into consideration the availability of transportation to and from the site. Parents who keep their youngsters out of school because they are unable to transport them are more apt to see that their youngsters attend the home study program if convenient transportation is available. Without this option, the home study program loses much of its potential for returning youngsters to the school system.

KEEPING CURRICULA CONSISTENT WITH DISTRICT GUIDELINES

It is important to provide an equal educational opportunity to all students enrolled in the home study program. This can be accomplished by supplying families with a curriculum that adheres to district guidelines, goals, and objectives. Although each family will want to structure educational goals individually to meet the needs of their youngsters, with proper planning and teacher assistance this can be accomplished within the framework of approved district curricula.

Consideration should be given to textbooks that have been used successfully by school department heads in the regular district schools. Other textbooks should not be used without the approval of the school board or the district's textbook committee. Supplementary materials brought in by the parents are generally very useful and can add a spark to the monotony of textbook reading. These materials should be closely scrutinized by the staff to be sure they conform to district policy.

CASE HISTORY OF CINDY: A STORY OF SCHOOL PHOBIA

The following case history will show how the home study program was used in one school system to prevent a troubled teenager from becoming a high school dropout.

Cindy was a slender, attractive girl with dark hair and a pretty face. Her parents were both college-educated and held well-paying jobs. At first, Cindy had an exemplary school attendance record and earned good grades.

The deterioration in her behavior was gradual. In the beginning, she would stay in school for two or three classes, then go to the nurse and claim she was feeling ill. The nurse would call one of the parents, who left work to come for Cindy. The frequency of this behavior slowly but steadily increased.

Then, just as gradually, a new pattern of idiosyncrasies began to creep in. Cindy would forget to set her alarm clock, arise late, and miss the bus. Her mother was forced to take Cindy to school more and more often. She missed so much school that her grades fell. Reprimands led to arguments, and the serenity of family life in the household plummeted.

Cindy's increasing tardiness and truancy led to many visits to the principal's office and finally to the school counselor. The counselor sensed there was more wrong than appeared on the surface and called for a parent conference in which she recommended psychiatric help. The parents requested time to think about the recommendation.

In the interim, Cindy's behavior got progressively worse until she finally refused to go to school at all. At this stage, she made no excuses for her behavior. Facing such an impasse, the parents wisely phoned the school counselor, who arranged for an appointment with the school psychologist. Cindy started her sessions that same day.

It was six months before the reasons behind Cindy's school phobia gradually emerged. During this period, Cindy was placed in the home study program. There, with guidance from the teacher and encouragement from the psychologist, her grades began to improve. She was learning again.

How Past Events Can Produce Phobias

Strangely enough, the events that triggered Cindy's phobia could very likely occur to numerous other persons without ill effect. Her problem was caused by an incident in her past that seemed insignificant at the time. Although it involved the entire family, all had taken it in stride and forgotten it, except Cindy.

During her final year in junior high, she had arrived home from school one day to find the front door locked. When no one answered her persistent knocks, she searched and found all the other doors and windows locked. When she tried to use the backup system her parents had devised and went to get a key from a close neighbor, the neighbor was nowhere to be found. She was all alone and there was no place for her to go. She lived miles from town and had no transportation.

Frightened, she sat on the front porch in the dark, with no house or street lights. She grew cold. The tears flowed just as her mother arrived in the car and pulled to a hasty stop.

Her mother apologized, then explained in hurried words why she was late. Cindy's brother had been in a car accident, and Cindy's mother and father had been detained at the police station answering questions. Cindy and her mother rushed back to the police station. There Cindy sat alone again, excluded from the conversation, cold, hungry, and ignored while her parents engaged in the routine of getting her brother released. No one gave a thought to Cindy's feelings during this whole time.

It was more than a year after Cindy's first visit before the psychologist arrived at the conclusion that the incidents of that particular day were the root cause of Cindy's problems and her reluctance to attend school. Cindy rebelled against going to school because of her subconscious fear that when she came home, no one would be there. The way to solve the problem was simply not to go to school. Cindy, of course, was completely unaware that the traumas of that particular day had affected her so drastically. The counselor immediately informed Cindy's parents.

The Home Study Program Keeps Cindy in School

Cindy remained in the home study program for the rest of the school year and part of the next. But identifying the problem was not in itself a cure. It took much work on Cindy's part, continued help from the home study teacher, and guidance from the counselor. Her parents, too, were diligent in their efforts to teach Cindy at home and keep her studies current. They also had adjustments to make, but teaching Cindy at home was their number one priority.

Attending regular school became a gradual process for Cindy, just as her truancy had been. She started with half a day. So successful was her rehabilitation that eventually she graduated with her own class.

How the Home Study Program Helped Cindy and Her Parents

In this case, the home study program was the perfect tool. Cindy's parents were able to fulfill their legal responsibility by keeping their teenage daughter in school while at the same time allowing her to be at home, as she requested. The open-ended program promoted a family rapport and included a series of productive counseling sessions that served to speed Cindy's cure.

The availability of the program was crucial. Without it, Cindy would have had to choose among several negative and unproductive alternatives that could have had a devastating impact on her life, as well as on her family. For example:

1. Cindy did not become a high school dropout, and she did not curtail her educational advancement.

2. The family was spared the disruption that would have ensued if Cindy had left school.

3. Cindy was not forced to go to school, which might have caused further emotional damage and mental anguish.

4. Cindy's parents were not forced to choose between their daughter's desire to learn at home and the compulsory attendance laws.

ENROLLMENT FORM FOR HOME STUDY PROGRAM

_____   _____   _____
Student's name   Birth Date   Age

_____   _____   _____
School District of Residence   Grade   Date Last Attended

_____   _____
Name of Parent or Guardian   Home Phone

_____
Address   (Number Street   Apt. #   City   Zip)

Reason for Request _____

_____

_____

_____

_____

Length of Time Requested _____

_____   _____
Signature of Parent or Guardian   Date

Educational Needs of Student _____

_____

_____

_____

_____

_____   _____
Signature of Director   Date

Individual Monitor in Addition to Parent and Program Director

_____   _____
Monitor's Name (Please Print)   Monitor's Title

_____   _____
Monitor's Signature   Date

Form 12–1

INFORMATION REQUEST FORM

Date Requested _____

To: _____

_____

_____

We would appreciate receiving information on:

_____   _____
Name of Student   Birth Date

Please enclose the following:

( ) Psychological evaluation   ( ) Medical records

( ) Health and development test   ( ) Educational records

( ) Hearing/audiological test   ( ) Vision test

( ) Speech and language test   ( ) Other _____

Send to:

_____   _____
School Name   Director's Name

_____
School Address

_____   _____
Requested by   Title

I hereby authorize the above-named (person, agency, doctor, hospital, or school) to disclose pertinent information that may be of value to the education of my child.

_____   _____
Signature of Parent or Guardian   Date

Form 12–2

HOME STUDY CONTRACT

Student _____ Grade _____

Term of Contract _____ Date _____

Statement of student's educational needs _____

_____

_____

Student's goals and objectives _____

_____

_____

Plan to be used by student to achieve goals/objectives _____

_____

_____

Materials and/or assistance to be used by student to achieve goals/objectives

_____

_____

_____

Time and frequency of meetings _____

_____

Method of evaluation _____

_____

Person(s), in addition to program director or parent, who are responsible for assisting student with the educational plan.

Name _____ Title _____

I agree to follow the Home Study Plan as described in this contract. I understand that upon satisfactory completion I will receive credit for work completed.

_____   _____
Student's Signature (when appropriate)   Date

I approve of my child's participation in the home study plan as described in this contract.

_____   _____
Signature of Parent or Guardian   Date

_____
Signature of Director and/or Supervisor

I understand that the supplies, materials, and equipment provided by the _____ public school system and/or _____ county superintendent of schools Home Study Program are the property of the program and utilized by each student on a loan basis. Upon leaving the program, or when materials and equipment are no longer being utilized, I agree to return all materials and equipment to the program facility.

If any materials or equipment are lost or damaged, I agree to pay replacement costs.

_____   _____
Signature of Parent or Guardian   Date

_____   _____
Signature of Student (when appropriate)   Date

Form 12–3

HOME STUDY TIME RECORD

Student's Name _____ Grade _____

Supervising Adult's Signature _____

Date/Time Record Submitted _____

Dates	Mon.	Tues.	Wed.	Thurs.	Fri.
Enter the number of minutes spent each day.					
Dates	Mon.	Tues.	Wed.	Thurs.	Fri.
Enter the number of minutes spent each day.					
Dates	Mon.	Tues.	Wed.	Thurs.	Fri.
Enter the number of minutes spent each day.					
Dates	Mon.	Tues.	Wed.	Thurs.	Fri.
Enter the number of minutes spent each day.					

Subjects at the elementary level are interrelated and therefore not separated for timekeeping purposes. It is understood that all subjects are incorporated in each week's lessons.

Total minutes _____ **School month** _____

Number of minutes required per day for this grade level _____

Total minutes divided by required minutes equals _____ days of apportionment attendance

Comments _____

_____

Form 12–4

HOME STUDY LOG

Student's Name _____ Grade _____

Supervising Teacher's Name _____

Home School Address _____

_____

Contact Dates | Comments

___/___/19___ _____

___/___/19___ _____

___/___/19___ _____

___/___/19___ _____

___/___/19___ _____

___/___/19___ _____

___/___/19___ _____

___/___/19___ _____

___/___/19___ _____

___/___/19___ _____

___/___/19___ _____

___/___/19___ _____

___/___/19___ _____

___/___/19___ _____

___/___/19___ _____

___/___/19___ _____

___/___/19___ _____

___/___/19___ _____

___/___/19___ _____

___/___/19___ _____

___/___/19___ _____

___/___/19___ _____

Form 12–5

Referral Sources and Guidelines That Will Help You Start New Programs in Your School or District

Alternative programs answer a social need in the school district and seek to establish a better balance of educational opportunities. Just because of their existence, they can make the community aware of the needs of school-age young people. These programs should be made available to all who can benefit from them.

The effectiveness of the public school system will be greatly improved if it offers pupils a variety of instructional programs. Students are individuals with different ways of learning and generally are more successful when they are allowed to select the program or school that suits them best.

An alternative school, or public school of choice, is a separate school or program within the district that

1. Is chosen with the cooperation of the pupil, the parent, or both

2. Offers an individualized education plan for each student

3. Allows flexibility in curriculum and teaching style, as determined by the education plan

4. Pursues the school district's educational goals, while at the same

time using learning techniques that are conducive to each student's individual learning style

All of the alternative programs discussed in this book are based on the concept of credibility. Credibility, in this context, encompasses those qualities that inspire the trust of students, parents, staff, and community. Such qualities include honesty, open-mindedness, and the ability to be nonjudgmental and accepting. True humanitarians possess empathy, compassion, selflessness, and self-respect; hence they can receive openly the communications of others.

Humanitarian qualities must be present in the people who operate the schools and those who are involved in running the programs. They are the essential ingredients in the success of any program that attempts to reach troubled young people. Without them, the program cannot have significant impact.

Credibility is not an inevitable part of a program; indeed, most programs do not have it at the outset. It is a goal toward which each program must strive. A staff that is dedicated to providing high-quality education will automatically strive for credibility, thus making the program meaningful for all who participate.

It is vital that teachers be given the materials, time, and opportunity to think and act creatively if the program is to be successful. To teach effectively in alternative education, a teacher must have highly developed personal skills in guiding and encouraging students. It is the responsibility of the administrators to ignite the spark that brings about change and to support new programs with aggressive leadership, clear definitions of purpose, and financial backing.

STEPS IN IMPLEMENTING A NEW PROGRAM IN YOUR AREA

Education is a national interest, a state function, and a local responsibility. Understanding the dropout problem and its cost to your state and the nation is not difficult. But difficulties do arise when people try to do something about the dropout crisis in their own school district.

When a group of educators or citizens decides that their public school system needs to provide more alternatives in education, the first question that arises is, "Where do we start?"

The first step in initiating a new program is a visit to the superintendent of schools or assistant superintendent of instruction. Present your idea to this person and seek permission to pursue the research needed to document a need for the program.

Discuss funding with the superintendent. If the program will be funded with district money, start to investigate ways to incorporate the new program into the existing budget. If state funds are needed, begin researching state laws for existing legislation that may provide money based on average daily attendance. Some districts have personnel who work exclusively with state and federal grants. These people know how to write grants that provide funds for new innovative programs.

Discuss the scope of your school board presentation. Some school boards prefer an initial presentation before research is done, then a follow-up presentation which includes all the details. Other school boards want all the information at the first presentation. Know your district board and follow the course of action that you feel is best.

The second step is to begin your research.

1. Become fully acquainted with the entire school district, both public and private sectors. Ask for a list of alternative programs that are now being offered in the district. Be sure your target population is not being served by a program that is already functioning. Address the specific needs of the students to be served.

2. Pinpoint target population and include statistics. (Example: _____ High School with an enrollment of 2000 has a 20% truancy rate because one parent families require older siblings to remain at home to care for younger children. Four-hundred youngsters could be brought back into the school system through alternative night programs). These are steps you can follow to identify your target population.
   a. Ask your superintendent if the district has completed a study on their dropout problem. Get a copy.
   b. Check with school counselors. They can provide names of students who are at risk or have already dropped out. Take time to check the cummulative files on these students. The files generally provide a history of school problems.
   c. State and federal governments keep statistics on the dropout rate. Write and ask for this information.
   d. Ask your state unemployment office if they have a record of applicants who have not completed high school.
   e. Make phone calls to parents whose children have dropped out and ask why their youngsters are no longer attending.

3. Ask the board of education to appoint an official committee (this can be the same group that initiated the idea) that can work together to gather data, develop ideas, and meet with the school board and/or city council. This committee should
   a. Prepare a definition of the problem. (Example: "One percent of the children between thirteen and eighteen years of age are school-phobic and tend to be truant. An independent study

program would provide an education for these youngsters while eliminating 1 percent of the truancy within the district.")

    b.   Identify the people who will be responsible for carrying out the program. (Example: teachers, counselors, principals, volunteers.)

    c.   Make a clear statement of objectives. (Example: "The course of study will meet school district curriculum guidelines. Students must attend x number of hours each school day.")

    d.   Submit a proposal for financing the program that shows district, state, and federal sources. (Consider private or state grants and federal funds.)

4.   Contact your district's state representative. The city or county library has the name and address of this person. Present the outline of the program and inquire about the possibility of a bill that could provide state funds for such a program.

5.   Contact the state department of education. The officials there are responsive to the individual, personal, and social needs of each student in every school in the state. They usually seek to improve existing programs and are open to suggestions for new programs.

It is important to remember that these steps take time. Do not become discouraged if the program is still in the planning stages after months of community-level and district-level work. It is up to you to keep trying. Remember, you can make your local schools into responsive institutions that meet the needs of your community and the demands of your young people.

Keep in mind that in most states school programs are funded on the basis of average daily attendance. Average daily attendance is computed for pupils engaged in any educational activity required of school-age children. Programs that bring dropouts back into the educational system increase the apportioned money received by their district.

If your state does not already have existing legislation covering the needed new alternatives, the initiation of new legislation or the written revision of existing laws to pave the way for their implementation may be originated with any group of citizens or special committee. A good idea is to use someone experienced in the field of law to draft the proposal. Another good idea is for the initiating group to approach their state senator or assembly person directly for his or her staff assistance. The resulting draft of such a proposal is referred to as a "bill" and is introduced in either the senate or assembly by a member of that body.

The bill is assigned an identifying number, e.g., AB123 (Assembly Bill 123), and routed to the house education committee. This committee reviews the bill, listens to pro and con arguments, then makes recommendations to the parent house. If the bill includes an appropriation of funds, it must also be referred to a finance committee. When both committees have made their report to the house, the pending legislation is voted upon. Upon passing into law the school district, wherein the initial proposal originated, is authorized to implement the program and funding is provided as outlined in the bill.

AVOIDING PROGRAM PITFALLS

Problems inevitably materialize when school administrators suddenly decide to implement a "money-making" alternative program such as a dropout retrieval program. Attempting to commence a new program without thorough planning can result in a runaway program that lacks credibility and results in failure to achieve the intended goal. It takes time to research proper procedures and guidelines and to hire and train staff. Some of the chief pitfalls to watch out for are

1. Overextended staff (too many students per instructor)
2. Undertrained staff (assigning staff members to duties that are beyond their competence)
3. Overenrollment (allowing enrollment to exceed available facilities and staff capabilities)
4. Insufficient background research

Dr. Edmund Vallejo, superintendent of the Pueblo School District, No. 60, Colorado, in his article "How to Curb the Dropout Rate"* suggests the following tactics in addressing the problem:

1. Reorganize the central administrative and professional staff responsibilities so that all district efforts are coordinated from one office.
2. Concentrate on new efforts and improving existing efforts.
3. Implement a new tracking system to assist staff in analyzing reasons for dropping out and to gather information about at-risk students.
4. Make the community aware of the economic and social implications of a continuing dropout problem and its long range impact on society if allowed to go unchecked; seek community support in initiating school-community partnerships to address the dropout problem.
5. Develop a mentorship program to help motivate students toward more positive goals.
6. Organize an ad hoc dropout prevention committee made up of interested community patrons, staff and students to advise and to

* Reprinted with permission.

monitor the district's efforts in dropout prevention, retention and retrieval.

MAKING USE OF EXISTING PROGRAMS

Obtain as much literature as possible from established programs. Program administrators are generally willing to share their knowledge with others. Use your phone to make an appointment with the head of an established program and plan a day to observe. During your observation, be sure to

1. Take clear and precise notes
2. Gather forms (ask if forms are copyrighted)
3. Ask for samples of curriculum materials and addresses of book companies that supply the types of materials you will need
4. Look at record-keeping procedures and ask questions about the state and local audits
5. Find out how the program was staffed and what qualifications are required
6. See if a consultant is available and if there is an organization that may be of help
7. Ask about the referral process: Where do students come from and who finds them? Find out what is done when a student is not successful in the program

Your peers are good allies. Never hesitate to ask for help. People enjoy sharing their success with others.

STATE-BY-STATE SURVEY OF ALTERNATIVE PROGRAMS

In 1985, I made a survey of alternative programs offered in the United States. For each state, I selected one of the most populous school districts and contacted the supervisor in charge of alternative programs. Correspondence often went from one individual to another within the district until someone with knowledge of alternative programs in their area was able to respond. The information relayed to me is reported below. However, it was impossible to verify the accuracy of the information I received.

The scope of the survey made it impractical to cover every city in every state. For this reason, only the most populous and largest school districts were contacted. Alternative programs are usually not as readily available in less populous areas.

Readers are urged to use discretion when interpreting the survey results. Each state is an individual entity with its own constitution and education guidelines. The descriptions, objectives, and names of the programs vary from state to state.

The chart in Form 13–1 shows an overview of the results of the survey. It is intended to be used as a guide only. A glance at the survey will show that districts in every state participating in the survey offer a number of alternative programs. To get more detailed information about program offerings, contact the largest school district in your state. Follow through by questioning community leaders, such as the mayor, council members, the police chief, and social workers. Use the telephone. It is your best ally.

FINDING THE CHILDREN WHO WILL BENEFIT THE MOST FROM ALTERNATIVE PROGRAMS

The use of a checklist such as the one shown in Form 13–2 can assist you in evaluating the behavior and development of individual children. When you are making the suggestion to a parent or guardian that an alternative program might help their child, it is best to be armed with information about the particular problem the child is having. The checklist can assist you here too. To confront parents with the bare and negative statement "Your child is having trouble in this school and needs a change" may put them on the defensive and cause unnecessary hostility. It is always better to be positive in your approach to placing children in alternative programs.

SUMMARY OF SURVEY RESULTS BY STATE

Alabama—The Birmingham public school system offers alternative programs called "magnet schools." They are listed as services, and although they are geared toward the average student, the magnet schools are open to all students and stress achievement in basic skills plus the development of special skills or talents. For further information about programs in Alabama, contact The Birmingham Board of Education, North Birmingham, Alabama 35203.

Alaska—Alaska offers an extensive program of individualized home independent study in grades one through eight. For statewide information contact The Department of Education, Juneau, Alaska 99801.

Arizona—Most alternative programs are offered statewide. The learning opportunity program encompasses an entire school site and provides lessons for students who are academically below or at their grade level. In-service training is provided to help teachers establish an instructional plan to meet learning needs. For statewide information contact Arizona State Facilitator, 161 E. First Street, Mesa, Arizona 85201.

Arkansas—The survey indicated that few alternatives for dropouts are offered. A parenting program is offered during school hours, but it does not provide child care facilities. For statewide information contact The Arkansas Department of Education, State Capitol Mall, Little Rock, Arkansas 72201.

California—California offers all the programs discussed in this book. The independent study program is incorporated statewide, as are continuation schools. Other programs can be found in various school districts. For statewide information contact The California Department of Education, Capitol Mall, Sacramento, California 94244.

Colorado—The survey indicated that fewer alternatives are offered than in many other states. However, one school district in Denver initiated a program for adolescent suicide prevention. The program was set up in local schools to spot potential problems among students. It is the first federally funded suicide prevention program in the country and is a model for other school districts. Adolescent suicide is the third leading killer of young people aged twelve to twenty-four, according to the National Center for Health Statistics. For statewide information about dropout prevention programs contact Superintendent of Schools, Pueblo School District No. 60, Pueblo, Colorado 81003.

Connecticut—A wide variety of alternative programs are available. Special education programs and the parenting program are situated at their own sites. A small, innovative high school is provided as an alternative to traditional high school. Similar to the continuation school, it provides a choice of learning modes and seeks to improve student's attitude toward learning. For statewide information contact High School in Community, New Haven, Connecticut 06511.

Delaware—Delaware provides a wide variety of alternative programs. In response to a high freshman dropout rate, a program was developed to create student awareness through weekly orientation classes. Potential dropouts are identified and placed in an aggressive outreach rehabilitation program. For statewide information contact Delaware State College, Dover, Delaware 19901.

Florida—Florida offers all alternative programs described in this book except independent study, as a substitute for regular school. It also provides an intervention program that helps prevent unproductive social behavior in high school students. For information about this program contact Project PASS, St. Petersburg, Florida 33705.

Georgia—Georgia offers most alternative programs with the exception of independent study as a substitute for regular school and the parenting program with a day care center. For information about alternative programs contact Georgia Staff Facilitator, University of Georgia, Athens, Georgia 30602.

Hawaii—The survey indicated that fewer alternatives were offered than in many other states. For full statewide information contact the Office of Instructional Services, 595 Pepeekeo Street, Building H, Honolulu, Hawaii 96825.

Idaho—No programs for pregnant minors are offered, but students with discipline problems are provided with some alternatives. For statewide information contact Idaho State Department of Education, Boise, Idaho 83720.

Illinois—In the Chicago School District, all alternative programs are offered, although independent study is not used as a substitute for traditional school but as an integral part of the overall education within the comprehensive school. For statewide information contact the Chicago School District, Chicago, Illinois 60604.

Indiana—Indiana offers a wide variety of alternatives, with the exception of the learning opportunity program. The independent study program is available to students over age sixteen only. Extensive vocational education programs are available. For statewide information contact State Department of Education, Indianapolis, Indiana 46206.

Iowa—In Des Moines, the high school district provides learning centers at separate sites for students with behavior and social problems. Most other alternative programs are also available. For statewide information contact Department of Public Education, Grimes State Office Building, Des Moines, Iowa 50319.

Kansas—A variety of alternative programs are available including the Diversified Educational Experiences Program for troubled youth with truancy and discipline problems. For full statewide information contact Project DEEP, Wichita Public Schools, Wichita, Kansas 67214.

Kentucky—Kentucky offers most of the alternatives described in this text. Independent study is used as an addition to regular school and not as a dropout retrieval program. For statewide information contact Department of Education, Capitol Plaza Tower Office Building, Frankfort, Kentucky 40601.

Louisiana—Louisiana offers a wide variety of alternative programs. There are few options for pregnant minors. For statewide information contact State Department of Education, Baton Rouge, Louisiana 70804.

Maine—Maine offers a wide variety of alternative programs. There are few options for pregnant minors and adult dropouts. For information regarding alternative programs contact Maine Facilitator Center, Auburn, Maine 04210.

Maryland—Maryland offers a variety of alternative programs. It does not offer independent study for purposes of dropout retrieval. It provides a complete program for pregnant minors. For statewide information contact Educational Alternatives, Inc., Port Tobacco, Maryland 20677.

Massachusetts—Most alternative programs are available. Independent study is very limited. Home tutoring is conducted after school hours by regular staff. The district provides a program emphasizing study skills for lifelong learning that increases the retention rate for students and increases competency in basic skills. For information about alternative skills programs contact Learning to Learn, Cambridge, Massachusetts 02138.

Michigan—The survey indicated that fewer alternatives were offered than in other states. For statewide information contact Michigan Department of Education, Lansing, Michigan 48909.

Minnesota—Minnesota offers a wide variety of alternative programs, all in joint-program settings with traditional schools. There are in-service training programs to help teachers establish alternative educational plans for troubled youths. Peer counseling for students is offered. For statewide information contact Focus Dissemination Project, Hastings, Minnesota 55033.

Mississippi—A wide variety of alternative programs are offered. For statewide information contact Mississippi Department of Education, Jackson, Mississippi 39205.

Missouri—In Kansas City, a wide variety of alternatives are available. The young pregnant minors program and the parenting program are housed together on their own site. For statewide information contact State Department of Education, Kansas City, Missouri 64501.

Montana—The survey indicated that fewer alternatives were offered than in many other states. The Great Falls District offers a teaching project designed to help elementary level students build basic skills, allowing them to achieve academic success in the higher grades. Contact Precision Teaching Project, Great Falls, Montana 59404.

Nebraska—There are a limited number of alternative programs available in

Lincoln. The independent study program is contained on its own site. For statewide information contact Nebraska Department of Education, Capitol Complex, Lincoln, Nebraska 89710.

Nevada—All alternatives are located together as a school within a school. Instructional clinics in nontraditional settings are used to help keep at-risk youths in school. For full statewide information contact the Nevada Department of Education, Capitol Complex, Carson City, Nevada 89710.

New Hampshire—The survey indicated that few alternatives were offered. For statewide information contact the State Department of Education, Manchester, New Hampshire 03101.

New Jersey—Most programs are available within the traditional high school setting. There is a vocational program for the mentally handicapped and a school-age parenting program. For statewide information contact the Family Learning Program, New Brunswick High School, New Brunswick, New Jersey 08901.

New Mexico—The survey indicated that fewer alternatives were offered than in other states. The vocational training program is quite extensive. For statewide information contact the State Department of Education, State Capitol, Sante Fe, New Mexico 87501.

New York—In Niskayuna Central School District #1, Schenectady, an ESEA Title III grant provided funds for an independent study project that enables students to work their way through the curriculum at their own pace. The objective of the program is to provide for more individualized student learning and more innovation in education. New York City offers extensive alternative programs. City-As-School program for at-risk adolescents links youngsters with the community in an effort to relieve the attrition rate. Contact City-As-School, New York City, New York 10014, or for statewide information, New York Education Department, Albany, New York 12234.

North Carolina—Most alternative programs are available. The young pregnant minors program is contained within its own site. For statewide information contact the North Carolina Department of Public Instruction, Raleigh, North Carolina 27613-1712.

North Dakota—Most alternative programs are available. Some districts provide in-service instruction to help teachers diagnose and focus on student learning disabilities. For statewide information contact Northwest Special Education, Columbus, North Dakota 58727.

Ohio—Ohio offers a wide variety of programs and thrives on strong community support for innovative education. For statewide information contact the Ohio Department of Education, Division of Inservice Education, Columbus, Ohio 43215.

Oklahoma—Oklahoma offers a wide variety of programs, and more than half have their own facility. Youth officers are available to review student cases. There is a program that provides individualized instruction for learning-disabled adolescents. For statewide information contact Oklahoma Child Service Demonstration Center, Cushing, Oklahoma 74023.

Oregon—Eugene offers a wide variety of programs. All alternative programs are located on high school sites. For full statewide information contact Columbia Education Center, Portland, Oregon 97266.

Pennsylvania—Pennsylvania offers an extensive list of alternative programs. Many schools offer a curriculum that uses alternative education instead of traditional methods. For statewide information contact The State Department of Education, Public Education Building, Harrisburg, Pennsylvania 17126.

Rhode Island—The Cranston School Department offers a wide variety of alternatives. The independent study program is available at parent's request. The pregnant minors program is located at the community agency. All programs are provided to the student in the least restrictive environment. There is also a community-based alternative high school. For further information on any alternative program in any city in Rhode Island, contact the Department of Education, 22 Hays Street, Providence, Rhode Island 02903.

South Carolina—Although there are a limited number of alternative programs, there are social workers available within the school setting to counsel troubled students. All alternative programs are housed on the regular school campus. For full information on statewide programs contact South Carolina Department of Education, Senate Street, Columbia, South Carolina 29201.

South Dakota—The survey indicated that fewer alternatives were offered than in other states. For statewide information on all programs contact the Division of Elementary and Secondary Education, Pierre, South Dakota 57501.

Tennessee—The survey indicated that fewer alternatives were offered than in other states. For statewide information contact the State Department of Education, Nashville, Tennessee 37203.

Texas—Texas offers an extensive list of alternative programs, and many are housed on their own campus. There are numerous excellent opportunities for young people seeking a different mode of learning. For full statewide information contact the Texas Education Agency, William Travia Building, Austin, Texas 78701.

Utah—Utah offers a wide variety of alternative programs, most on school sites separate from the traditional campus. For full statewide information on programs contact the Utah State Office of Education, Salt Lake City, Utah 84111.

Vermont—The survey indicated that fewer alternatives were offered than in many other states. For statewide information contact the Vermont Department of Education, Montpelier, Vermont 05602.

Virginia—Many of the alternative programs presented in this book are offered. The pregnant minors program and the vocational education programs are extensive and located on their own sites. For statewide information contact the State Department of Education, Capitol Square, Richmond, Virginia 23219.

Washington—The Seattle Public School District offers an extensive list of alternative programs. For full statewide information contact the State Facilitator, Highline School District #401, Seattle, Washington 98166.

West Virginia—West Virginia offers extensive opportunities in special education. Most other alternative programs mentioned in this book are available. For statewide information contact the West Virginia State Department of Education, Charleston, West Virginia 25305.

Wisconsin—Wisconsin offers a wide variety of alternative programs and an extensive independent study program. For full statewide information contact the Department of Public Instruction, Madison, Wisconsin 53707.

Wyoming—Wyoming offers fewer alternative programs than other states. For statewide information contact the State Department of Education, Hathaway Building, Cheyenne, Wyoming 82002.

REPRESENTS DISTRICT CONTACTED IN THE STATE OF	HOME TEACHING	INDEPENDENT STUDY	PARENTING	PREGNANT MINORS	FREE COUNSELING	S.A.R.B.	C.A.R.B.	LEARNING OPPORTUNITY	SPECIAL EDUCATION	VOCATIONAL PROGRAM	OTHER
ALABAMA	X			X*	X			X*	X*	X	X
ALASKA		X									
ARIZONA	X		X	X*					X*	X*	X
ARKANSAS	X		X		X				X	X	
CALIFORNIA	X	X*	X*	X*	X	X	X	X	X*	X*	X
COLORADO	X				X					X	X
CONNECTICUT	X	X		X*	X				X	X*	X
DELAWARE	X			X*	X				X*	X	X*
FLORIDA	X		X*	X*	X			X	X*	X*	X
GEORGIA	X			X	X				X*	X	X
HAWAII											X
IDAHO	X			X	X	X	X		X	X	
ILLINOIS	X	X	X	X*	X	X	X	X	X	X	
INDIANA	X	X	X	X	X				X	X*	
IOWA	X		X*	X*	X			X	X*	X*	X
KANSAS	X			X*	X				X	X*	X
KENTUCKY	X	X		X*	X			X	X*	X*	
LOUISIANA	X	X*			X*	X	X	X	X*	X*	
MAINE	X	X			X	X	X		X	X	
MARYLAND	X		X*	X*	X				X	X	X*
MASSACHUSETTS	X	X			X		X		X*	X	X
MICHIGAN	X		X*	X*					X*	X*	
MINNESOTA	X		X	X				X	X	X	
MISSISSIPPI	X	X			X				X	X	X
MISSOURI	X		X*	X*	X				X*	X	X*
MONTANA	X			X*	X				X*	X*	X
NEBRASKA	X	X*							X	X	
NEVADA	X									X	X
NEW HAMPSHIRE	X									X	X
NEW JERSEY	X			X*	X				X	X	X
NEW MEXICO	X			X*	X				X	X*	
NEW YORK	X	X	X	X	X				X	X	X
NORTH CAROLINA	X			X*	X	X	X	X	X	X	X
NORTH DAKOTA	X	X		X*	X	X	X		X*	X	
OHIO	X	X*	X		X	X	X		X	X	X*
OKLAHOMA	X	X*		X*	X			X	X	X*	X
OREGON	X			X	X				X	X	X
PENNSYLVANIA	X		X*	X*	X				X	X	X
RHODE ISLAND	X	X		X*	X				X	X	X
SOUTH CAROLINA	X				X					X	X*
SOUTH DAKOTA	X				X					X	X*
TENNESSEE				X*	X				X	X	
TEXAS	X	X	X*	X*	X				X*	X*	
UTAH	X	X*	X*	X*					X*	X*	X*
VERMONT	X	X			X				X	X*	X*
VIRGINIA	X			X*	X	X	X		X*	X*	
WASHINGTON	X	X*	X*	X*	X				X	X	X*
WEST VIRGINIA	X		X*	X*	X				X*	X	
WISCONSIN	X	X*		X*	X				X	X*	X
WYOMING	X	X			X				X	X	X

* Own site/extensive program

LEARNING PROBLEMS OBSERVATION CHECKLIST

To be filled out by
referring Teacher/Principal

DATE _____

STUDENT _____ GRADE _____ TEACHER _____

Check areas you see/feel are a frequent area of concern:

MOTOR DEVELOPMENT

_____ 1. Has poor posture
_____ 2. Holds chalk/pencil awkwardly
_____ 3. Strokes too heavily or lightly
_____ 4. Works very slowly on simple pencil-paper tasks
_____ 5. Is easily fatigued

VISUAL PERCEPTION

_____ 1. Difficulty discriminating differences in color, form, shape, size
_____ 2. Difficulty recognizing what is missing
_____ 3. Frequently loses place on work page
_____ 4. Difficulty with visual memory
_____ 5. Difficulty interpreting reversible letters or words

VISUAL MOTOR

_____ 1. Difficulty staying on line or within boundary lines
_____ 2. Poor orientation of drawings on page
_____ 3. Poor spacing of drawing/writing
_____ 4. Difficulty in copying
_____ 5. Cramped or sprawled writing
_____ 6. Reverses or rotates angles in letters or words

SPACIAL ORGANIZATION

_____ 1. Untidy with clothing, desk, etc.
_____ 2. Inconsistent hand preference
_____ 3. Confusion of left and right
_____ 4. Difficulty with sequence

REGULATION BEHAVIOR

_____ 1. Distractibility—has difficulty staying on task
_____ 2. Hyperactivity—restlessly active
_____ 3. Hypoactivity—lethargic
_____ 4. Perseveration—repeats excessively some words or actions without apparent reason; gets stuck on some letter, sound, or word; seems to need security of repeating same word or action over and over again

_____ 5. Disinhibition—grabs; puts hands where they don't belong; little regard for danger; can't wait, runs out of line; has to be first; little regard for regulations

_____ 6. Impulsivity—exhibits irresistible reactions to stimuli

_____ 7. Inconsistent performance from hour to hour, day to day

LANGUAGE DEVELOPMENT

_____ 1. Difficulty recognizing differences in sounds or words presented verbally

_____ 2. Difficulty understanding verbal directions

_____ 3. Difficulty expressing thoughts

_____ 4. Difficulty classifying or categorizing words

_____ 5. Difficulty finishing incomplete words

_____ 6. Difficulty blending separate parts of a word into a whole word

_____ 7. Difficulty with sentence structure or grammatical form

_____ 8. Difficulty reproducing from memory sequences presented verbally

PERSONALITY DEVELOPMENT

_____ 1. Daydreams

_____ 2. Is preoccupied with certain themes, such as violence, desertion, etc.

_____ 3. Has exaggerated emotional responses (cries too easily, laughs too loud)

_____ 4. Exhibits nervous traits and mannerisms such as nail-biting, thumbsucking, pencil-chewing, etc.

_____ 5. Needs constant approval

_____ 6. Resists changes

_____ 7. Seems to have difficulty in being accepted by peers

_____ 8. Acts overly bold and aggressive

Form 13–2

Index